Volume 28

NATIONAL WAGES POLICY IN WAR AND PEACE

NATIONAL WAGES POLICY
IN WAR AND PEACE

B.C. ROBERTS

Routledge
Taylor & Francis Group

LONDON AND NEW YORK

First published in 1958 by George Allen & Unwin Ltd

This edition first published in 2025
by Routledge
4 Park Square, Milton Park, Abingdon, Oxon OX14 4RN

and by Routledge
605 Third Avenue, New York, NY 10158

Routledge is an imprint of the Taylor & Francis Group, an informa business

© 1958 George Allen and Unwin, Ltd

British Library Cataloguing in Publication Data
A catalogue record for this book is available from the British Library

ISBN: 978-1-032-81770-5 (Set)
ISBN: 978-1-032-80414-9 (Volume 28) (hbk)
ISBN: 978-1-032-80423-1 (Volume 28) (pbk)
ISBN: 978-1-003-49679-3 (Volume 28) (ebk)

DOI: 10.4324/9781003496793

Publisher's Note
The publisher has gone to great lengths to ensure the quality of this reprint but points out that some imperfections in the original copies may be apparent.

Disclaimer
The publisher has made every effort to trace copyright holders and would welcome correspondence from those they have been unable to trace.

National Wages Policy
in
War and Peace

B. C. ROBERTS

Reader in Industrial Relations
in the University of London

Ruskin House
GEORGE ALLEN & UNWIN LTD
MUSEUM STREET   LONDON

FIRST PUBLISHED IN 1958

PRINTED IN GREAT BRITAIN
in 10 pt Times New Roman type
BY SIMSON SHAND LTD, LONDON, HERTFORD AND HARLOW

To
R.W. and D.C.

PREFACE

NATIONAL WAGES POLICY IN WAR AND PEACE

production of this book I am deeply grateful, but I must make quite clear to the reader that I alone am responsible for everything that has finally been written.

London, November 1957.   B.C.R.

Economic conditions can change surprisingly quickly and it could be possible that when this book appears in print the problem of preventing inflation is no longer uppermost in the minds of the public and the authorities. But even if the main problem has once again become that of stimulating the economy to the maximum level of employment and output, the lessons to be drawn from the experience of the post-war decade will still be valuable since the signs of inflation may rapidly begin to reappear. This is my excuse for attempting to draw together in a short book the experience of national wage policies gained in war and peace under a variety of different economic and social conditions. The conclusions to my mind are extremely clear and they may be summed up as showing that a centrally administered national wages policy cannot be relied upon as a means of preventing inflation. It follows that economic stability must be maintained in some other way. This book seeks to indicate how this may be achieved with the minimum interference with free collective bargaining if all parties, Government, trade unions and employers exercise their power with responsibility.

I would like to express my thanks to the editors of the *Oxford Economic Papers*, *Economica* and *Lloyds Bank Review*, for giving me permission to use material from articles first published in these journals. Chapter 5 is based upon an article which appeared in the *Oxford Economic Papers*, Vol. IV, No. 2, July 1952. The substance of Chapter 8 was drawn from an article in *Economica*, August, 1957, and sections of Chapter 11 from an article in *Lloyds Bank Review*, April, 1957.

I have been greatly assisted in the writing of this book by the generous help of many of my colleagues who are members of the Senior Common Room at the London School of Economics and Political Science. I would like to mention Professor E. H. Phelps Brown in particular, since he has read every chapter and given me the benefit of his critical judgment. I owe far more to him than this brief acknowledgment can ever suggest. I am much indebted to Mrs I. J. Boyer for her efficient typing and to Mrs M. H. Klonarides and Mrs K. Gothill for the graph on page 65. In the onerous task of reading and checking the manuscript and proofs the work done by my wife has been indispensable. To all of those who have helped me with the production of this book I am deeply grateful, but I must make quite clear to the reader that I alone am responsible for everything that has finally been written.

London, November 1957   B.C.R.

CONTENTS

CHAPTER 1

Economic Aspects
of the Problem

Wages have been a crucial issue in the making of economic policy for
at least seven centuries. It is not intended, however, to review, in this
book, the course of wage policy in war and peace over the long span
of history since 1351, when Edward III laid down in the Statute
of Labourers day and yearly wages and empowered Justices of the
Peace to hold quarter sessions to ensure that the Act was carried out.

The problem of our day is to discover the appropriate wages policy
to ensure (*a*) a rising national income, (*b*) that a fair share of the
nation's wealth goes to workpeople, (*c*) the maintenance of full
employment and (*d*) stable prices and a healthy balance of payments
with the rest of the world. It is possible that an examination of the experience of a number of countries during the past twenty years may
throw enough light at least to illuminate the nature of the difficulties
that have to be overcome.

Since the sweeping away of wage regulations, with the advent of
laissez-faire in the eighteenth century, the settlement of the price of
labour in Britain has been a matter decided in the main by private
negotiation uncontrolled by the State. Insofar as public policy has
been concerned with wages, until the last twenty years, it was confined
to the establishment of minimum wages. The object of state intervention in the field of wage determination has been to provide support for
the trade unions in their efforts to achieve minimum wage levels that
would abolish 'sweating' and at least enable a worker to enjoy a
reasonable subsistence standard. In Britain this aim was achieved
through such instruments of public policy as the Fair Wages Clause
in Government contracts, and through Trade Boards—later Wages
Councils—which were empowered to fix legally enforceable minimum
wages and certain conditions of employment.[1] The Cotton Manufacturing (Temporary Provisions) Act empowered the Minister of
Labour to make a statutory order legally imposing the wage levels
agreed upon by collective bargaining on all employers in the appropriate section of the cotton industry. No attempt was made to lay

[1] See *Industrial Relations Handbook*, HMSO.

down and enforce by law a national minimum wage binding upon all employers. This notion was frequently discussed by trade unions, but was generally thought to be too rigid to secure the best results.

Many other countries without Britain's long tradition of trade unionism and collective bargaining were prepared to give the State authority to fix minimum wages by law. The first country to enact minimum wage legislation was New Zealand, where the Industrial Conciliation and Arbitration Act was passed as early as 1894. Australia followed suit and in 1904 established a Commonwealth Court of Conciliation and Arbitration, with powers to make legally binding awards on the parties to an industrial dispute. The principle of 'authoritative control' had first been introduced into Australia by the State of Victoria in 1896 and had been adopted by several other States before the Federal legislation was passed.[1]

The great depression led to the passing of legislation in the United States which established a national minimum wage for a maximum working week for all labour engaged in inter-state commerce or the production of goods for inter-state commerce. Minimum wage laws had been passed in a number of States at an earlier date than the Federal law, but had been declared unconstitutional by the Supreme Court.[2]

Canada, South Africa, France, Germany, Austria, Czechoslovakia, Norway, Hungary and a number of other countries had all introduced some form of legal minimum wage before the second World War.[3] It could, therefore, be said that public interest in wage policy, the world over, insofar as it was expressed in the actions of governments, as well as of trade unions, was concerned with the laying down of a floor below which no man's income from paid employment should be allowed to drop. With the outbreak of the second World War public policy at once became more concerned about establishing maximum wage levels rather than minima.[4] The wage problem was stood on its head, for the new problem was how to prevent wages from going up too fast rather than to prevent them from falling.

The Impact of Trade Unionism on Wages

Although before 1939 public policy was mainly confined to the regulation of minimum wages, there was considerable controversy among economists, both as to the effect of fixing a minimum wage by law

[1] Cf. O. de R. Foenander, *Towards Industrial Peace in Australia.*
[2] *Adkins* v. *Children's Hospital.*
[3] J. H. Richardson, *The Minimum Wage.*
[4] There had, of course, been some concern about wage inflation in previous wars.

and also as to the effect of trade unions on the general level of wages. This controversy continues unabated, though it has changed somewhat in character as the dimensions of the problem have altered.

There are, broadly speaking, two views about the impact of the unions on the course of economic events. One view may be summarized as the significant-impact view, and the other as the insignificant-impact view. Or, to put the matter another way, one group of economists see the trade unions as the principal factor causing inflation, distorting the pattern of incomes and the allocation of resources.[1] The other group see the unions as playing a relatively passive role, accommodating their behaviour to the push and pull of more fundamental market forces and tending to smooth out imperfections rather than to make them worse.[2]

The holders of any particular economic theory are inevitably greatly influenced by their social and political predilections. Those who believe that the trade unions have had a powerful impact on wage changes during the past twenty years fall into two groups. The first group consists of strong supporters of a *laissez-faire* society who see the trade unions as the devil incarnate, bent on destroying individual freedom to be rich or poor. This ambition, to people who are well-to-do, seems usually to be a supreme evil. In their opinion trade unions have become all-powerful and are responsible for forcing up wages to levels which make inevitable price rises and all the troubles consequent on this course.

Closely allied to this group, though for entirely different reasons, are the ardent supporters of trade unionism who believe that the trade unions have had a very significant effect on wage levels. They hold this view, because to do otherwise would question the *raison d'être* of trade unionism, but they part company with the former group on their analysis of the causal connection between the movement of wages and price changes. In the eyes of the majority of trade unionists, price changes are caused by the expansion of profits, not wages; if, it is indignantly argued, employers did not insist on maintaining constant profit margins it would not be necessary to raise prices.[3] Some trade unionists, whilst not dissociating themselves from the view that profits are also a cause of inflation, accept the argument

[1] See C. E. Lindblom, *Unions and Capitalism* (1949); Henry Simons, *Economic Policy for a Free Society* (1948).
[2] See L. G. Reynolds and C. Taft, *The Evolution of Wage Structure* (1956); W. A. Morton, 'Trade Unionism, Full Employment and Inflation', *American Economic Review*, March 1950.
[3] This point of view has been provided with a sophisticated theoretical support by T. Barna in his pamphlet *Profits during and after the War*, Fabian Society.

that wage pressure is the principal cause, and seek a remedy in a national wages policy.[1]

On the opposite side of the table in this debate sit those who hold that the fundamental cause of inflation lies in the Government's economic policy. The behaviour of the Government is derived from a large number of factors, of which trade union pressure is only one. Rising wages are, it is argued by this school of thought, a function of the general level of demand; they are pulled up by the competitive bidding of employers seeking labour, which, because of full employment, is in short supply, in order to satisfy the demand for products generated by the general level of economic activity. Collective bargaining, on this analysis, is simply the instrument through which the more fundamental forces in the economic situation are transmitted.

Wage Levels and Unemployment

Since many people find the notion that trade unions are not the primary cause of inflation repugnant to their common sense, it is necessary to examine the impact of the union on wage levels at rather greater length. In order to do this systematically the influence of the union on wages will be considered in both the short and long run under conditions of unemployment as well as full employment.

It has been noted that in the past hundred years, in which employment has been less than full, wages have not tended to fall proportionately to the amount of unemployment. This so-called elbow-joint behaviour, or, as it is sometimes expressed, 'ratchet effect' of money wages, has been attributed to the growth of trade unionism. It is suggested that the unions are able to push up money wages in times of full employment, when, with no reserves of labour, their bargaining strength is greatly enhanced, and are then able to maintain sufficient strength to prevent wages from falling as far or as fast, as they otherwise might, in times of economic depression.

Looking back over the statistics of wage changes it does appear as if something rather like this has happened. However, doubt is cast as to whether the effect observed is due to the advent of trade unionism, since Professor Phelps Brown and Miss Sheila Hopkins have shown that wages of craftsmen in the building industry have behaved in this way for seven centuries.[2] That is to say, the ratchet effect apparently occurred in some sectors of employment long before collective bargaining became the normal method of wage fixing.

It was the contention of many economists, prior to the second

[1] Cf. C. Geddes, 'Sharing Prosperity's Cake', *Sunday Times*, August 25, 1957.
[2] E. H. Phelps Brown and Sheila V. Hopkins, 'Seven Centuries of Building Wages', *Economica*, August 1955.

World War, that the stickiness in the downward adjustment of wage rates, attributed to the power of the unions, was the prime cause of the failure of the economy to respond to the natural pulls of the market towards the full employment equilibrium. If employers were compelled to pay more for labour than would have been the case under free market conditions, then they would have to cut their costs by reducing their demand for labour. It was assumed that this was the only way in which normal profits, that is to say, the rate of profit which would just keep them in business, could be maintained.

This static and rather over-simple analysis was severely criticized from several directions. Lord Keynes pointed out that simply to cut money wages, as was suggested by the critics of collective bargaining, would not affect the level of effective demand directly, but only through having some effect on the rate of interest.[1] Since this same effect could be achieved by increasing the quantity of money, to do it through cutting wages was to follow the more difficult of two paths that would ultimately lead to the same result. As a matter of practical policy it was no use expecting a fall in money wages as sharp and severe as was necessary to stimulate an expansion of investment. What was more likely to occur was a steady sagging of the price and wage levels as employers and workers tried to make up their minds as to what was likely to happen next. This was precisely the kind of circumstance that led both unions and employers to welcome minimum wage policies, in the hope that the knowledge of a limit to the decline would encourage confidence. It was this situation that led Keynes to postulate the view that money wages were rigid and, therefore, it was futile to expect real wages to decline by way of a fall in money wages.

To prevent wages from falling would not, however, stop prices from falling, since the effect of holding wages up would be to reduce the demand for labour. In other words, aggregate demand for products would fall via the employment effect of the wages policy. Thus it was possible to be caught in a situation from which it was extremely difficult to escape without outside assistance. That assistance Keynes saw as being promoted by the Government through its fiscal and monetary policies.

Wage Levels and Full Employment
Though it is doubtful whether it is possible for trade unions to bring a recession to an end by their wage negotiations, once expansion is under way trade union pressure might influence the movement of wages in a number of directions. Employers might be persuaded by

[1] J. M. Keynes, *The General Theory of Employment, Interest and Money* (1936).

the threat of strike action to increase wages at an earlier stage than would have been the case under non-union conditions. If employers were concerned to fulfil contracts they might be particularly vulnerable at the critical stage of an upturn in economic activity. They might, therefore, be willing to allow their profits to be squeezed by the unions in the knowledge that there would be a good chance of recouping the loss as demand expanded. The rise in wages and the ensuing demand for consumer goods could stimulate further expectations of expansion and encourage buying in advance of price increases, thus adding to the upward movement.

On the other hand, the institutionalizing of wage fixation might well have the opposite effect. Wages under collective bargaining are not settled on the spot by piecemeal agreement between an employer and a worker, but as the result of a deliberate bargaining process which is conducted through a complicated system of negotiating committees. The process of settlement is not, therefore, a rapid one, and it is possible that collective bargaining, through the lags that it imposes, acts as a drag on the upward movement of wages in a boom.[1] The fact that employers are willing to pay more than the negotiated wage rates in order to obtain the labour that they require points to a situation in which wage rates are lagging behind the levels that they would spontaneously reach as a result of market pressures.

Attempts have been made to measure the effect of trade unions on wage movements, but the results are far from conclusive.[2] In periods of economic expansion wages would rise simply from the demand and supply position, and it is impossible to separate the impact of the union from the other factors at work in the labour market. Even when non-union firms or industries are discovered it is difficult to draw definite conclusions, since the effect of union organization and collective bargaining in other sections cannot be entirely isolated. For instance, it is well known that many non-union firms pay above union rates in order to avoid having to negotiate with a union. Since they must never allow their rates to fall behind unionized firms they are linked effectively to union negotiated wage rates.

[1] A. T. Peacock and W. J. L. Ryan, 'Wage Claims and the Pace of Inflation', *Economic Journal*.

[2] See C. Kerr, 'Wage Relationships—the Comparative Impact of the Market and Power Forces', in *The Theory of Wage Determination*, Ed. Dunlop (1957), L. G. Reynolds and Taft, *op. cit.*; N. Goldfinger and E. M. Kassalow, 'Trade Union Behaviour and Wage Bargaining', *New Concepts in Wage Determination* (1957); H. A. Turner, 'Trade Unions, Differentials and the Levelling of Wages', *Manchester School of Economic and Social Studies*, September 1952.; H. M. Levinson, *Unionism, Wage Trends and Income Distribution, 1914–1947* (1951).

Wages and Prices

The fact that wage movements and price movements are linked together does not mean that price changes are solely determined by wage change. Many other factors enter into the pattern of relationships that finally result in prices going up or down or just remaining stable.

In an economic situation that is in a dynamic equilibrium, that is to say, one in which the flow of income, expenditure and saving just balances the output of goods and services, wage increases will not be inflationary if they do not exceed the rate at which production is rising. If wage advances outpace production then prices are bound to rise, unless there is an increase in the amount of savings that just equals the difference between the amount of goods and services available at the current price levels and the amount of money available for spending. If, therefore, net production is rising at two per cent per year, in order to maintain a stable price level wages must not exceed this amount plus an addition for savings.

It is possible, however, that other factors will change, and this may permit a rate of wage increase that is faster or make necessary a slower rate of wage increase. The most important of these factors is the terms of trade. If the economy is, like Britain's, one in which foreign trade plays a very large part, changes in the price of imports relative to exports will make a considerable difference to real incomes.

If the price of imported raw materials, manufactures and foodstuffs is falling, this will make available more resources at current price levels, so long as prices for exports are not affected to the same extent. Thus, a shift in the terms of trade in favour of Britain would permit a larger rate of wage increase without having any effect on home prices. This would hold good so long as the increase in home wage costs did not exceed the fall in import costs and did not result in a fall in the aggregate income for British exports.

If, on the other hand, the terms of trade turned against us, and therefore imports became more expensive in relation to exports, it would be necessary to reduce wage costs per unit of output and total income by an amount equal to the rise in the total cost of imports if prices were to be kept stable. Real wages would, in other words, have to fall; if this could not be achieved by way of wage reductions, then internal prices would rise and the fall in real incomes would be brought about in that way.

As an alternative to adjusting incomes to the terms of trade and the balance of payments situation resort could be made to alteration of the value of the pound sterling. This method of adjusting the inflationary pressures generated by full employment is not, however,

B

one that can be lightly embarked upon by a country which is at the centre of a huge banking system like the sterling area. The effects of sudden adjustments in the value of the pound are always serious for a country in Britain's position. What is more important, however, is that devaluation of the pound would not protect the British consumer from the facts of economic life. If Britain is inflating at a faster rate than the rest of the world there is no way in which the British people can be ultimately saved from their folly, other than by exploiting the colonies by blocking their drawing rights on the gold and dollar reserves of the sterling area; by the receipt of loans—which is only putting off the evil day of reckoning, or by receiving gifts and living the life of a feckless, pitiable, charity-seeker.

Possible Forms of Attack on Problem
Clearly if a country like Britain is to avoid the constant menace to her position as a great trading nation which any adverse balance of payments and low reserves presents, inflation must not be allowed to run its insidious course unchecked. There are a number of ways in which the problem of inflation can be attacked and each raises its own economic, social and political problems. Fundamentally, what has to be done is to bring spending into line with the supply of resources.

Before 1914 there was no conscious policy for maintaining the economy in equilibrium, other than that produced by the Bank of England in the exercise of its responsibility for maintaining the gold reserves at an adequate level by means of changes in the Bank Rate. It was believed that the economic system was a self-regulating instrument that should not be interfered with. After the first World War it was still thought that the economy tended naturally towards a full employment equilibrium and that the Gold Standard acted as an automatic stabilizer. Though considerable doubt has been thrown on the alleged simplicity of the Gold Standard mechanism and the way in which it actually worked, shifts in the gold reserves could eventually lead to the cure of an inflation. Since a country in an inflationary situation would probably have an adverse balance of payments it would be losing gold, and the central bank would have to raise the Bank Rate to check this outflow. A rise in the Bank Rate would lead to a contraction in credit and investment demand would be reduced. As a consequence unemployment would be created and prices would begin to fall. The countries receiving gold would be experiencing exactly the opposite effects; they would be expanding their supplies of money, unemployment would be falling and prices would be rising. It was believed that these movements would go on until an international equilibrium had been reached; thus every time the equilibrium was disturbed it would be restored ultimately by the operation of the Gold Standard.

This is not the place to go into the breakdown of the Gold Standard. It is enough to note that no country was prepared to go on allowing its internal prosperity and level of employment to be determined by some factor, such as the flow of gold, over which it had little or no control.[1] In its place an elaborate insulating mechanism has been created, but ingenious as this is, it cannot protect countries that are greatly dependent on international trade from the effects of a fundamental unbalance in their economic situation.

Preventing spendable incomes from outstripping the availability of goods and services is, therefore, a matter of internal policy which cannot be shirked by reference to the sins of other nations. It is also in the best interest of every section of the community that the problem should be resolutely tackled.

One way in which inflation could be stopped is by restricting the supply of money, by deliberate action of the Government, to such an extent that prices no longer rise. The monetary and fiscal techniques which can be used to achieve a situation in which the aggregate supply of money is brought into balance with the supply of resources are well known, but they also involve the danger, if pressed hard enough, that unemployment may be increased and the growth of output might be checked. Because of the political implications of economic policies which appear deliberately to reduce economic activity, and create unemployment, modern Governments are understandably reluctant to make full use of the powerful anti-inflation weapons that are at their command. This reluctance is reinforced by the genuine difficulty that no one can predict with certainty what the critical level of employment is. At what level of unemployment will wage and price increases be checked? Will it be at three, five or ten per cent? Since this question is of such fundamental importance it requires the most careful consideration, in the light of experience at home and abroad.

These difficulties have led some economists to observe that a policy of full employment, in effect, involves putting the economy on to a labour standard.[2] What is meant by this phrase is that when wages rise, instead of the employer having to find some way of keeping his costs steady, he is able to pass the increase on to the consumer by way of higher prices. He is only able to do this, however, because the credit system has expanded and increased the total supply of money.

[1] H. W. Arndt, *The Economic Lessons of the Nineteen Thirties*, Oxford (1944).
[2] J. R. Hicks, Presidential Address to the Economics Section of the Royal Society. *Economic Journal*, September 1955.

If this had not happened the increase in wages and prices must have been at the expense of some other sector of the economy. There would have been some redistribution of income but the higher prices would eventually have slowed down the demand, and prices would then have settled at a stable level; if, however, the quantity of money is constantly expanded when prices rise, then since aggregate demand never receives a check, the only limit to the upward climb is that which is set by the effect on the balance of payments.

It would be possible for wages and prices to rise to some extent without any increase in the aggregate quantity of money, by means of an increase in the velocity of circulation. There is, however, clearly a limit to a movement of wages and prices autonomously financed by a greater velocity of circulation, and a curb on the supply of money must, sooner or later, bring a check to the growth in demand. Whilst, therefore, it may be plausibly argued that a wage-price spiral can be generated without an increase in the supply of money, it is extremely unlikely that it could continue for long without a quantitative expansion in the volume of credit and cash in circulation.

A tight monetary policy is not the only way in which the problem of inflation can be attacked. It is possible to erect a system of direct controls of wages and prices that act as a dam across the flow of money incomes. This can be done at various stages. The most comprehensive system of controls would be by way of a national wage, salary and dividend policy, which fixed these at levels determined by some authoritative body. In this way the amount of income allowed through the sluice gates would be determined by the general state of the economy. In addition, the price of goods could be fixed by an administrative authority and supported by subsidies. Prices could, of course, be administered, as indeed they were during the war and for some years after, separately from a system of income controls.

The difficulty about this type of attack on the problem of inflation is that it fails to remove one of the principal causes of the excess demand for resources, namely the over-supply of money. The pressure of demand will, in fact, be increased by the extent to which prices are prevented from rising. In this situation there is almost certain to develop a black market, since there is a premium to be gained from evasion of the controls. This problem is inevitably made very much worse in a situation in which price controls exist but wages are left free.

If the policy is really successful in choking off demand by stabilizing wages, as production overtakes the controlled incomes, it is almost certain to bring about some fall in the level of employment. Thus the net effect of a policy of controls that succeeds in stopping the inflation will be some increase in the number of unemployed. It would, therefore, in the end have the same effect as the policy of restricting the supply of money.

The policy of checking inflation by administrative controls over incomes has the added disadvantage of requiring the establishment of a national income structure. Since incomes must bear the right relation to each other, if they are to fulfil the basic economic function of allocating resources to where they are required, it would be necessary to work out the levels at which each wage, salary and dividend should be fixed. This would be no easy matter, and the process would involve the most profound political and social repercussions.

Any attempt to evolve a detailed wage policy would almost certainly require the exercise of control over every facet of wage payment. Collective bargaining would, therefore, have to be restricted to the limits set by the nationally determined requirements. The alternative would be to adopt a policy of labour direction. If this were followed then differentials would become less important as the means of allocating the supply of labour. Either course would meet with enormous difficulties in Britain in peacetime. Almost certainly there would be a great conflict with the trade unions, who would be likely to resist the encroachment on their freedom to negotiate on behalf of their members.

A more profitable approach to the problem of inflation might be found in the use of investment controls. The control of capital issues, building and the investment programmes of nationalized industries could play a valuable part in an attack on inflation. Any attempts, however, to build in such controls as permanent features of the apparatus of economic administration would have far from inconsiderable drawbacks. Since these controls would operate in a haphazard fashion they would, if used as a regular instrument, tend to have a distorting effect on the pattern of economic growth. Great care would have to be taken to see that the cure did not prove to be worse than the disease.

The problem of inflation may also be tackled from the side of production. A rise in output could be as effective as a fall in income in bringing demand and supply into balance. An increase in production is not, however, in itself disinflationary, as many persons seem to think, since it may have been achieved at the expense of higher costs. Higher production obtained as a result of adding to the aggregate level of demand may well be less than the rise in incomes that will have been induced. Rising production is only an antidote to inflation when the real product is greater than the total costs incurred. There is no reason, however, why productivity should not be substantially increased, since it can be assumed with absolute certainty that the utilization of resources falls a long way short of the optimum in any economic situation, even in one that has operated at the level of 'full employment' for many years. It must also be borne in mind that one of the most effective ways of obtaining higher productivity might be a slight reduction in the pressure of demand, since this is likely to make resources more mobile and so better utilized.

The attack on inflation from the side of raising productivity is closely connected with the question of wage policy from the point of view of incentives. To be really effective any national wage policy would have to make provision for incentive payments; this, however, presents a great difficulty, since such payments are extremely difficult to police. They could provide merely a means of evading the controls, and so undermine the policy.

Wage Policy and Social Justice

The supporters of a national wage policy have not rested their case simply on the contribution such a policy might make to finding a solution to inflation and increasing productivity; they have also been concerned about the question of equity in the distribution of income. They are, therefore, faced with the problem of deciding what is a fair income and how this distribution may be brought about. Unfortunately, there are no absolute criteria of social justice to which appeal can be made. There is, therefore, no agreed standard of reference by which this income or that income can be tested for fairness. Everybody has his own notion of fairness and it is one of the fundamental prerogatives of a democratic society that he should be able to express his point of view by refusing to work at the price offered. In the end, in a democratic society, the yardstick of fairness is a rough and ready utilitarian calculus.

The share of the national income going to wages, salaries, interest and dividends appears to be determined by powerful economic forces. Labour's share of the national income has apparently fluctuated a good deal, within certain fairly narrow limits, in most countries for which data exist.[1] In Britain, during the past seventy years, the share of wages in the national income has fluctuated between 36 and 42 per cent; if salaries are added the share of earned income is raised to between 55 and 66 per cent. The average income per head of wage earners has, however, risen relatively much more than the average income of other groups, since the proportion of wage-earners to the rest has fallen. The change in the ratio of the average income of the

[1]Clark Kerr, 'Labour's Income Share and the Labour Movement', in *New Concepts in Wage Determination* (1957).

occupied non-wage-earner to that of the wage-earner has been calculated by Professor Phelps Brown and Miss Sheila Hopkins to have fallen from 7.46 in 1881 to 3.35 in 1948.[1] This course of events could rightly be described as 'remarkable' since it has been brought about mainly by the processes of social growth.[2]

The change in the distribution of income which has come about during the past seventy years has not been by any means mainly due to the advance of trade unionism. Only in certain economic circumstances have the unions been able to secure a greater share of the national income for labour.[3] These circumstances have occurred when the employers have felt compelled to grant wage increases, but have not been able to pass on the increase in wage cost in the form of higher prices. Thus unions have been able to squeeze profit margins in times of 'hard' markets; that is, when business conditions have been such as to prevent employers from raising prices. In times of 'soft' markets, that is to say, in conditions of demand that would permit price increases, the unions have not been able to alter the share of the national income going to labour by means of collective bargaining. Thus, paradoxically, unions have been more successful in obtaining a larger share of the national income in periods of depression when they appear relatively weak, than in periods of boom when they seem to be at their maximum strength.

Salaries, as a proportion of the national income, have risen from 15 per cent to 23 per cent since 1880, but the average income of salaried workers, per head, has probably fallen relatively to the rise in income per head of wage-earners.[4] The narrowing of the difference in the incomes of wage and salary earners has been brought about, in the main, by the great advance in education, which has vastly increased the supply of persons capable of doing salaried jobs.

The proportion of the national income accruing to home produced profits was practically the same in 1950 as it was in 1880, but the share of rents in the national income had fallen dramatically from one-sixth to one-twentieth.[5]

It is possible to shift the distribution of income by controls and taxation; in Britain the post-tax share of wages in the national income is substantially greater than the pre-tax position. In the Soviet Union the proportion of the national income accounted for by wages and

[1] E. H. Phelps Brown and Sheila V. Hopkins, 'Wage Rates in Five Countries, 1860–1939'. *Oxford Economic Papers*, June 1950.
[2] *Op. cit.*
[3] E. H. Phelps Brown and P. E. Hart, 'The Share of Wages in the National Income', *Economic Journal*, June 1952.
[4] Phelps Brown and Hart, *op. cit.*
[5] Phelps Brown and Hart, *op. cit.*

salaries is, by comparison with the democratic nations, such as America, Australia, Britain and Canada, extremely low, amounting to only 35.7 per cent in 1948.[1] The proportion of the national income going to wages and salaries has been kept deliberately low in the Soviet Union by a Government determined to advance capital construction at the expense of current consumption. In Britain the effect of Government interference with the distribution of income has been to bring about greater equality and to promote increased consumption.

The Limits of Wage Policy

No Government can avoid having a wage policy. It may be a policy which involves no direct interference with the mechanism of wage fixing, but even non-intervention is a policy. Since Governments must be concerned about the general level of economic activity, they must also be concerned about the general wage level. The critical question is whether the Government should normally confine its policy to the exercise of influence on the level of wages by means of its monetary and fiscal policies.

The Governments of Britain, America, Australia, Sweden and Holland have each, in their own fashion, interfered with the freedom of collective bargaining. The degree of intervention has been in Britain the least and in Holland the most far-reaching. In Britain and America intervention has been looked upon as a regrettable necessity rather than as a desirable activity on the part of the Government. In both Australia and Holland, on the other hand, wage determination has come to be accepted as a matter of such fundamental public importance that it cannot be relegated to the autonomous activity of employers and trade unions.

For Australia and Holland wage policy is not an issue of concern to the authorities only in times of economic and social crisis; the public interest in wage determination is, in their view, a continuing one and must at all times be looked after by a responsible central agency.

The purpose of any wage policy is to achieve the economic and social goals set by the society concerned. In our day and age this involves the establishment of a general level of wages that is consistent with full employment and a stable price level. The level of wages must, therefore, be determined by the economic need to allocate resources to where they are required and to provide such rewards as will ensure that measures are utilized with maximum efficiency. At the same time the pattern of incomes generated by the various forms of economic

[1] Clark Kerr, *op. cit.*

activity must reasonably supply a basic notion of fairness, agreed upon by society; otherwise the danger of breakdown will always be acute and the goals will not be reached.

The adoption of a national wage policy which involves the making of key decisions affecting wages at a central point does not mean, in a democracy, that the interests of the various groups involved can be lightly regarded. In a free society wage policy is not something that is determined by a small body of planners, remotely situated in a closely guarded Kremlin, which can be imposed by an autocratic oligarchy and administered through pliant managers of state-owned enterprises with the support of subservient trade unions. In a democracy social institutions, such as trade unions, are repositories of independent power that cannot be over-ridden with ease. An important feature of a free society is that industrial ownership is not entirely concentrated in the hands of the State. So long as a large sector of industry remains in private hands, the policy of a Government can be opposed and even rendered nugatory if it violates the interests of managers and men. Thus the limits of Governmental authority are reached much earlier in a democracy than in a dictatorship.

Wage policy must inevitably be set in the framework of social and political institutions, traditions and practices of each nation state. This is not to say that institutions cannot be changed, old traditions abandoned and new practices adopted, but that the process of change is not simply that of working out logically on paper the most perfect wage policy and then putting it into effect. It is a matter of moving towards the chosen goal by tolerably effective expedients. The way in which democracies have sought to meet the challenge of wage policy in recent decades will be examined in the following chapters.

CHAPTER 2

British Wage Policy
in Wartime

The problem of preventing a runaway inflation, if war should break out, had been the subject of much discussion by Government departmental committees before 1939. Proposals for the control of wages, prices and the direction of labour had been carefully considered, but when the war did start the Government had no firm policy on labour matters ready to pursue.[1] The attitude of the Ministry of Labour was the principal reason why the Government had no cut and dried plans which could be put immediately into effect. The Ministry of Labour, though not to the same degree the partisan custodian of labour interests as the American Department of Labour, was highly sensitive to the reflexes of the trade unions. By tradition the function of the Ministry was to advise, guide and cajole unions and employers, rather than to exercise administrative control over them, and it was reluctant to embark on a policy of direct interference with the normal voluntary pattern of making industrial arrangements. The Ministry believed that the loyalty and patriotic self-interest of the trade unions could and should be relied upon. It was not without evidence to support this point of view, since during the summer of 1939 the Amalgamated Engineering Union and the Engineering and Allied Employers' Federation had entered into an agreement to relax traditional customs and practices that might hinder production in the event of a national emergency. Steps had also been taken to set up, if it proved necessary, a National Joint Advisory Council, composed of representatives of the unions, employers and the Government. It would be the duty of this body to discuss every issue of concern to labour that was posed by the exigencies of the war situation, with the object of agreeing on the measures that should be taken to secure the most effective prosecution of the war.

First Steps towards a Wages Policy
Prices rose sharply in the first three months of the war and the

[1] W. K. Hancock and M. M. Gowing, *British War Economy*, HMSO (1949), p. 59 *et seq.*

Government began to show signs of anxiety about the economic situation. On December 6, 1939, the Chancellor of the Exchequer, Sir John Simon, addressed the National Joint Advisory Council on the subject of the wage-price spiral. Sir John sought to convince the trade union representatives that it was in their interest not to press for wage increases in an attempt to avoid a drop in real wages.He urged the unions and employers to exercise restraint and slow down the tempo of wage advances. This theme was taken up again by the Prime Minister in a speech, also broadcast to the nation, that was delivered at the Mansion House on January 9, 1940. Mr Chamberlain was at pains to convince his listeners that the war could not be financed by taxing the rich still further, and that the tying of wages to the cost of living would only 'give violent impetus to the vicious spiral of the alternate rise of wages and prices'.[1] The Prime Minister's speech lacked positive proposals and it provided no reassurance to the growing weight of professional opinion that the Government was as dangerously muddled and complacent in its approach to economic affairs as it appeared to be in its organization of military activities.

Powerful articles setting forth a coherent economic policy had appeared in *The Times* on November 14 and 15 and on January 5, under the signatures of J. M. Keynes and R. H. Brand. A few weeks later J. M. Keynes published at greater length a masterly analysis of the economic problem which faced the Government and a positive policy to deal with the situation. There was impressive unanimity among economists as to the nature of the problem, though there were differences of opinion as to the best method of dealing with it. The most important thing that was required was political wisdom and courage to take the necessary steps to ensure first public understanding and then agreement to the measures that were required to maintain economic stability.

It was generally agreed that the vast increase in Government expenditure would generate a rise in incomes, while at the same time the production of goods for civilian consumption would be severely curtailed. Inevitably there would be a huge rise in prices unless demand was somehow restricted. 'We shall have to combine control of wages, saving, taxation, rationing and some rise in prices in order to keep consumption within the needed limits,' wrote R. H. Brand.[2]

Undoubtedly Keynes could justly claim credit for the level of technical understanding of the inflationary problem. The task now was to

[1] *The Times*, January 10, 1940. An emergency Budget had been introduced in September 1939; income tax had been raised from 5s 6d to 7s 6d; death duties by 10 per cent and excess profits levied 60 per cent.
[2] *The Times*, January 5, 1940.

secure public acceptance of an effective policy. Keynes was deeply concerned that even in wartime the essential features of a free society should not be abandoned. His aim was 'to devise a means of adapting the distributive system of a free community to the limitations of war'.[1] This objective, he was acutely aware, could only be achieved if the majority of the people, and especially organized labour, were convinced that the sacrifices which they would be called upon to bear were fairly distributed. He indignantly repudiated the charge that he was bent on fighting totalitarianism with totalitarian methods. 'No criticism could be more misdirected,' he wrote. 'In a totalitarian state the problem of the distribution of sacrifice does not exist. That is one of its initial advantages for war. It is only in a free community that the task of government is complicated by the claims of social justice.'

Just before Keynes published his pamphlet *How to Pay for the War*, the Government decided to try to prevent a general rise in wages by extending the food subsidies, which they had hesitantly introduced as temporary measures, in order to prevent the cost of living index from suddenly shooting upwards. Keynes welcomed this decision as a prudent stopgap that would gain time for the introduction of a more comprehensive policy. Taken by itself, the policy of subsidies was the opposite of a solution. 'In making money go further it aggravates the problem of reaching an equilibrium between the spending power in people's pockets and what can be released for consumption.'[2] Somehow the means had to be found for withdrawing sufficient purchasing power to keep the total level of demand commensurate with the supply of goods at prevailing price levels.

If people would save enough, then the problem would be solved, but it was obvious from experience that as individuals they would not be able to decide on the level of savings necessary to avoid inflation, and, even if they ought to economize, it was doubtful if they could be relied upon to make the sacrifice. The link between immediate self-interest and the ultimate logic of the collective consequences was too attenuated to ensure that inflation could be prevented by relying on voluntary savings alone. Keynes, therefore, concluded that voluntary private savings should be supplemented by a system of compulsory saving or a deferred income scheme.

To the idea of deferred pay Keynes added a second and third principle. The second principle was that the bulk of the new taxes that would be required to finance the war should fall on the income groups with above £250 per year; while the third principle was the

[1] J. M. Keynes, *How to Pay for the War*, p. 7.
[2] *Ibid.*, p. iv.

establishment of a national minimum better than had ever existed. The third principle would be given effect by the provision of family allowances, since the burden of the cost of living bore most heavily on the larger families. In addition there should be available a minimum ration of consumption goods at a low fixed price.

Thus Keynes combined in a unified set of proposals a method of preventing inflation which at the same time achieved a substantial degree of social reform. The element of radical social reform contained in Keynes's scheme for soundly financing the war effort was taken a stage further with his conception of using the fund of deferred income as an anti-slump device in the post-war years. (He did not conceive of full employment continuing without a check for more than a decade after the end of hostilities.)

In order to meet criticism that the Treasury would have difficulty in discharging its obligation to pay back the deferred income—a difficulty which Keynes himself believed to be non-existent—the futher radical proposal of a post-war capital levy was made. This device would not only be useful in raising the capital required to pay off the deferred income debt; it would also be useful for scooping up whatever increment due to wartime fortune escaped the excess profits tax net.

By this combination of devices Keynes hoped to win the support of the trade unions; indeed, acceptance of the scheme by them was the *sine qua non* of its validity. However, since Keynes was sufficiently aware of the danger of promising more than events might make possible, he cautioned against specific pledges to hold the cost of living at a given level. He also realized that the trade unions could not be held to any specific pledge that they would not in any circumstances press for an increase in wages. But he did believe in the possibility of persuading them that it would be in their best interests to agree to a policy of the kind that he suggested and to refrain from pressing for increases in wages on grounds of the cost of living so long as the basic index number was kept from rising.

Keynes' proposals were too radical for the Treasury to swallow at once and since they attracted little support from organized labour they stood small chance of being adopted *in toto*. The analytical methods adopted by Keynes in his pamphlet were, however, to exercise a profound influence on the economic direction of the war effort. The deferred income proposal was converted into a system of post-war credits based on the amount of income tax paid. The notion of a minimum ration at a fixed price within reach of the poorest sections of the community also became a basic feature of wartime social policy. Family allowances had to wait until the end of war before they were introduced. The capital levy suggestion was never put into effect, partly because the Government's economic policy manifestly spread the burdens of sacrifice fairly. Whatever might have been the case in the first World War it was clear in the second World War that the rich had not waxed fat at the expense of the poor. Indeed, quite the opposite was true; the war brought a tremendous speeding up in the trends towards greater social equality, both in terms of income and status.

The Attitude of the Trade Unions

The unions were intensely suspicious of the Chamberlain Government; they did not believe that the interests of workpeople would receive fair consideration from an administration which was at heart anti-trade union. The gulf that had to be bridged before genuine co-operation could be achieved was bluntly expressed by Ernest Bevin in his union's journal a few weeks after the war began. Trade unionists would not sit on any committee if invited as an act of patronage; ministers and departments would have to cease treating them with a scarcely veiled contempt. Without the support of the trade union movement the war could not be won; that support could only be fully mobilized if the 'powers that be' accepted the principle of equality, 'Equality not merely in the economic sense, but in conception and in the attitude of mind of those in power . . .'.[1]

The Prime Minister was left in no doubt as to the views of the Trades Union Congress, and eventually instructions were issued to every Government department that the unions were to be consulted on all questions affecting the interests of their members and the war effort. The unions were not, however, prepared to enter into any agreement or to accept any Government policy that would limit their freedom to make wage claims. In the opinion of the General Council any attempt to control movements for wage increases was impracticable and undesirable. At the same time the General Council assured the Government that unions would not seek to exploit the situation. However, they were not prepared to extend to employers the freedom which they claimed for their own activities. They urged on the Government a policy of controlling prices and profits and they were in favour of ensuring fair distribution by a rationing system.

With the fall of Mr Chamberlain and the advent of the coalition, in which Ernest Bevin and other prominent trade union and labour leaders were to play leading roles, the responsibilities of the trade union movement for the successful prosecution of the war effort became more direct. The military situation was desperate, and Mr

[1] T & GWU Record, October 1939.

Bevin at once sought to remove wage problems from the field of controversy so as to avoid any distraction from the immediate task of building up Britain's badly mauled armed forces. A smaller body than the National Joint Advisory Council was established to advise the Government, and its first task was to consider whether it would be possible to make some general regulation treating each industry alike, or, if this were not feasible, whether it would be possible to make arbitration compulsory if the normal negotiating machinery had failed to produce a settlement. Bevin's suggestion that wages should be stabilized at prevailing levels and subject to review at intervals of four months was turned down by both the employers and the TUC. It was agreed, however, that a National Arbitration Tribunal should be set up, since it was imperative that there should be no stoppage of work owing to trade disputes.

On the basis of this agreement the Minister was given power by Order in Council to establish an independent Tribunal, whose decisions would be legally binding as an implied term of the contract of employment; to prohibit strikes and lockouts; to require employers to observe recognized terms and conditions of employment. The ordinary arrangements for settling wages were to remain operative, but in case of deadlock either party was free to notify the Minister of a trade dispute; it then rested with the Minister as to whether he referred the dispute to the NAT or to appropriate voluntary machinery. If the voluntary machinery failed to achieve a settlement, or there appeared little prospect of an agreement being reached in a reasonable time, the reference might be cancelled and the Minister could refer the dispute to the NAT. If the Minister did not refer a dispute to the NAT within twenty-one days of notification the parties were legally free to cease work.

No attempt was made by the Government to influence the decisions of the National Arbitration Tribunal by direct instruction, but in July 1941 it was decided to issue a White Paper to bring about a better understanding of the Government's price stabilization policy. The White Paper was a carefully worded document, but it did not require a highly subtle intelligence to appreciate that it was suggesting to the Tribunal and other wage fixing bodies that general wage increases should be avoided. However, it conceded that 'the maintenance of wages and employers' remuneration at a reasonable level should be achieved as far as possible by improvement in the efficiency of production by the joint efforts of employers and workpeople. At the same time there may, consistently with these considerations, be proper grounds for adjustment of wages in certain cases, particularly among comparatively low paid grades and categories of workers, or for adjustment owing to changes in the form, method or volume of production.'[1]

The TUC reacted sharply to what the General Council sensed was an attempt to establish an administrative control of wage changes by influencing the decisions of the National Arbitration Tribunal. In a long statement to the 1941 Trades Union Congress, Sir Walter Citrine made the position of the unions quite clear. They were not prepared to accept wage stability, since 'a stabilization of wages would mean that we would be expected to accept a depressed standard of life for the rest of the War'. Nor were the unions prepared to allow 'bureaucrats in Government Departments to interfere any more than is necessary with the functioning of the well-tried wages and disputes settling machinery we have established'.[2]

However, in rejecting the timidly advanced notion of a wage policy, determined through the National Arbitration Tribunal, the General Secretary of the TUC left the door open for the receipt of further proposals. 'We have stood for no interference with the wage system. We repeat that, but it does not mean to say that our General Council is not prepared to look at any practical scheme that is put before us to try to solve this very anxious difficulty. One thing we are certain of: that the solution will not be found in trying to interfere with the system which has been established and which, on the Government's own testimony, has worked so admirably.'[3]

The buffeting which the Government's kite received shook the confidence of those who were convinced that wages ought now to be brought under tighter control. The authors of the official *History of the War Economy* have revealed that there were anxious discussions and deep heart-searchings about the Government's wage policy, among Ministers in the latter months of 1941.[4]

Ernest Bevin, however, stood in the way of any attempt to force the trade unions to accept the direct control of wages by a Government agency. In the event the Government made no further moves to persuade the unions to change their attitude. The policy of stabilization based on subsidies and price controls was continued and, in conjunction with rationing, high levels of taxation, and the willingness of employers, unions and general public to behave with restraint and responsibility, the Government managed to keep the economy remarkably steady.

[1] *Price Stabilization and Industrial Policy*, Cmd. 6294.
[2] TUC Annual Report, 1941.
[3] *Ibid.*
[4] Cf. Hancock and Gowing, *op. cit.*

Changes in Wage Rates, Earnings and Prices

Wage rates lagged behind the rise in prices during the first two years of the war, but earnings soon began to gallop ahead. By July 1941 earnings had risen by 43 per cent above the level of October 1938, but wages were only 18 per cent higher. This development reflected the switching of workpeople into the defence industries, lengthened hours of work, and an increase in the number of workers paid by results. Earnings continued to rise faster than wage rates until 1944; in that year the demand for labour began to slacken and as the end of the war came in sight during the early months of 1945 there was a sharp cut back in production which checked the rise in earnings.

It can be argued that from the point of view of inflation changes in wage rates are the most important feature since these reflect an actual change in basic labour cost for a time period worked.[1] Earnings, on the other hand, reflect to a considerable extent an actual rise in production. This argument, according to the authors of the official *History of the War Economy*, was often used by Ernest Bevin to justify non-intervention with the fixing of wages.[2] The Minister of Labour stated with his usual bluntness that he didn't care how much a man drew in wages so long as it did not come from higher rates, but higher earnings. Since the rise in earnings was not due solely to harder work and higher output, as Bevin apparently imagined, the validity of the argument cannot be accepted without qualification. Of greater importance, however, from the point of view of inflation, was the fact that the continuously rising earnings were not being matched by any increase in the quantity of goods available for civilian consumption. What was, perhaps, most astonishing, in the circumstances, was that retail prices rose, on average, by only about 7 per cent per annum.

When the Government finally made up its mind to accept subsidies 'on a clear and avowed principle, instead of a mere drifting from a temporizing expedient',[3] it was decided to aim at stabilizing the cost of living index at between 125 to 130 of the pre-war level. This objective was not realized, as Table I shows. But considering all the circumstances, the rise in the index over the whole period of the war was remarkably modest. The relatively slow rise in prices as shown by the index was mainly due to the success of the Government's financial policies. It was also due in part to the nature of the index,

---

[1] Cf. G. Penrice, 'Earnings and Wage Rates since 1938', *London and Cambridge Economic Bulletin*, September 1952.

[2] Hancock and Gowing, *op. cit.*, p. 339.

[3] R. S. Sayers, *Financial Policy, 1939–45*, London (1956).

C

TABLE 1

	Wage Rates		Earnings		Retail Prices Index	Annual Sum of Small Savings £m
1938	100	Oct.	100	Oct.	100	57
1939	101	July	–	–	102	103
1940	110	July	130	July	119	454
1941	118	July	143	July	130	616
1942	124	July	160	July	139	612
1943	130	July	176	July	143	733
1944	136	July	182	July	146	716
1945	143	July	180	July	148	676

Source: *London and Cambridge Economic Bulletin*

the manipulation of food subsidies, price control and the utility schemes.[1]

The cost of living index was based on a pre-1914 survey of consumer expenditure and in effect it measured the basic items of food, rent and rates, clothing and fuel and light. A new index, based upon a survey made in 1938, was in the process of construction when the war broke out. That it had not been introduced turned out to be a stroke of fortune, since the 1914 index probably came closer to measuring the pattern of wartime consumption than a more up-to-date index would have done.

The policy of subsidies and price controls would have failed to hold the index down had not direct and indirect taxation skimmed off a large amount of the purchasing power secured by workpeople in the form of higher earnings. Heavy as the burden of taxation was, it would not have been in itself adequate to keep prices from rising at a much faster pace had not the recipients of the earnings wisely saved on a considerable scale. Small savings rose from £103 million in 1939 to a peak of £733 million in 1943; this result was to no small extent due to the savings schemes adopted, with the support of the trade unions, in most workshops.

Sir Walter Citrine, speaking to the 1941 Trades Union Congress on the subject of wages policy, concluded with a statement on the vital importance of voluntary savings. The problem which faced the trade union movement, he told his audience, 'will ultimately be determined by the measure to which we have succeeded in putting back into the war effort the maximum amount of savings—and I repeat, if voluntary saving is found to be inadequate, then we shall be faced with other and more stringent means. It is no use shutting our eyes to it. It is palpable it will come.' The trade unions had not at first been enthusiastic supporters of the savings movement, since they feared that wartime savings would be regarded as a reason for denying a

[1] See W. K. Hancock and M. M. Gowing, *op. cit.*, and R. S. Sayers, *op. cit.*

man his entitlement to unemployment benefit. It was only after Sir Kingsley Wood had promised the unions that up to £375 'lent to the nation' would not be taken into account in any means test, that the TUC agreed to give unqualified support to the savings campaign.

Direction of Labour

If the Government was prepared to leave the settlement of wages to normal methods of voluntary negotiation, supported by compulsory arbitration as a last resort, it was not prepared to leave the allocation of labour to the natural mobility induced by the pulls and pushes of the labour market. Vast numbers had to be called to the armed forces, the defence industries had to be manned, and labour had to be moved when and where required by the exigencies of the war.

At the outbreak of the war there were no plans ready to put into effect to secure the movement of labour that would be required. The philosophy of the Ministry of Labour was that ' "individualism" would do the job'.[1] A faint-hearted Control of Employment Act was passed in September 1939, but it was not until after the fearful events of 1940 and the change in the leadership of the nation that a vigorous attack on the problem really began. The weakness displayed by the Ministry of Labour in this early period of the war arose from its fear of the trade unions and its belief that any attempt to pursue a policy of industrial conscription would lead to a dangerous climate of industrial unrest. With the appointment of Mr Bevin as Minister of Labour a fresh attack was made on the entire manpower problem.

The Minister of Labour had power, under the Emergency Powers Act of 1940, to direct any person to perform any task that might be required, at any place and under specified terms and conditions of employment. No Minister in modern British history had ever been given such drastic powers over the lives of persons and immense care had to be taken to see that these powers were exercised fairly. It seems that the Minister was, if anything, over cautious in the use of his powers to direct and coerce.[2] He succeeded, however, in mobilizing both for the services and for essential work the manpower of the country to a degree unreached in any other nation.

The majority of workers were persuaded to enter war industry by factors other than the direction of the Ministry of Labour; the opportunity of making a good wage was not least important of the attractions to war work. The Government was not, however, inclined to look upon wages as a suitable instrument for inducing labour to move to the essential industries, since they feared that the policy of

[1] Hancock and Gowing, op. cit., p. 61.
[2] Ibid., p. 312.

stabilization might be jeopardized by competitive bargaining. The higher earnings that were obtainable on munitions work and on the many special 'rush jobs' that were called for by the services, undoubtedly proved an effective attraction. In the case of mining and agriculture the Government saw to it that wages were raised to a sufficient extent to maintain the required labour force in these two vital industries. Though the Government exercised an influence on the course of wage rates and earnings during the war, the important changes that occurred in the relative levels could not be attributed to a deliberate policy.

TABLE 2
Changes in Wage Rates
August 1939 = 100

	March 1942	July 1945
Bricklayers	118	133
Bricklayers' Labourers	123	141
Printers' Compositors	113	125
Dock Labourers	115	123
Engineers' Fitters	120	141
Engineers' Labourers	126	154
Shipbuilders	129	156
Railwaymen	121	141
Cotton	135	172
Wool	129	146
Local Authorities	121	143
Trains	124	139
Lorry Drivers	119	135
Boots	121	137
Confectionery	121	159
Tailoring	123	153
Shirts	123	153
Tobacco	123	132
Coal	140	193
Agriculture	173	201
Weighted Av.	127	152
Cost of living	129	134

Source: *London and Cambridge Economic Bulletin*

The war brought about a notable narrowing in the differentials previously enjoyed by the skilled craftsmen. Since wage claims tended to be on a cost of living adjustment basis they were usually demands for a flat rate increase. In 1939 about 1½ million workers were covered by sliding scale agreements, but during the war the iron and steel, cotton and other important industries decided to adopt this system, bringing the number of workers whose wages went up automatically with the cost of living to almost three million. The result of these developments was inevitably to reduce the percentage differences between the various levels of the wage structure. This effect could be justified on grounds of equity, and it reflected both the general egalitarian trend of the time as well as the growing strength and significance of the General Labour unions which organized the lower paid, less skilled workers. The narrowing of differentials that occurred during the war left behind a problem for the years of peace that was not to be easily solved. When the direction of labour does not exist, workers must be attracted to jobs by the lure of wages and conditions of employment. Under conditions of strong trade unionism and full employment it is not an easy matter to adjust the pattern of differentials, after six years of wartime distortion, to the needs of a peace-time economy.

Industrial Unrest

Strikes and lockouts were illegal, with minor exceptions, during the war. Nevertheless strikes occurred; indeed the number of strikes tended to increase, and went up by leaps and bounds in 1944 and 1945. The number of working days lost did not increase in the same proportion; they were, with the exception of 1944, on the average slightly lower than in the immediate pre-war years.

Almost all of the strikes that occurred were unofficial. They were not launched by the unions as part of a calculated policy to secure higher wages, but were called by local groups with some grievance which they felt was not being given the attention it deserved either by their employers or the unions. Faced by these outbreaks the authorities generally took the view that it was not wise to mobilize the force of the law to put them down. So long as the unions were not violating the no-strike order it was better to tackle the problem by conciliatory methods than by using the power of coercion. This policy of handling illegal stoppages in a tolerant, cautious fashion enabled agreement to be reached with the unions to maintain the National Arbitration Order after the war was over. The employers were less convinced of the merit of retaining compulsory arbitration, which could be enforced against them, but not against their employees. They were not disposed, however, to abandon compulsory arbitration, since that would have been an encouragement to the unions to return to the strike as a weapon in collective bargaining. So long as the strikes that occurred were unofficial, it was not the essence of wisdom on the part of employers to suggest a change that would free the unions from the ambiguity in their position.

The general success, which it might be claimed attended the efforts of the Government to prevent runaway inflation, was not achieved

TABLE 3

	Number of strikes	Working days lost (000)
1919	250	7,713
1920	248	17,508
1921	170	77,961
1922	169	1,387
1923	197	1,212
1924	204	1,628
1925	175	3,740
1926	69	146,456
1927	115	695
1928	100	461
1929	162	666
1930	158	671
1931	155	2,859
1932	115	292
1933	117	455
1934	150	373
1935	233	1,385
1936	290	969
1937	470	1,501
1938	374	701
1939	417	612
1940	386	508
1941	482	338
1942	555	862
1943	862	889
1944	1,275	2,495
1945	1,319	644

Source: *Ministry of Labour Gazette*

without a cost that had to be paid later. The savings which had been such an important factor in reducing the pressure on prices during the war were banked ready for release when the war should be over. It was recognized that this stock of purchasing power might create an inflationary problem, but it was beyond the danger of a post-war boom, which it was assumed could be handled by a continuation of wartime controls, that most people were fixing their gaze. It was not anticipated that continuing peacetime inflation would be the major problem that it has become. The general assumption of the professional economists and laymen alike was that it would not be easy to maintain full employment for any length of time. If the accumulated war savings could be released at a steady pace, rather than in a sudden burst, they would be a valuable stabilizing factor in the peacetime economy that, on previous experience, would be more threatened by deflation than inflation.

Another aspect of wartime financial policy, which could undoubtedly be claimed as a great success, but which was to present problems in the post-war period, was the low rate of interest which had been maintained. The Government's decision to borrow at three per cent meant that the cost to the nation that would have to be met by future taxpayers was very much less than it would have been by the canons of the first World War. Cheap money inevitably involves the creation of credit in such quantity that the supply of money is large enough to meet the demand for it at that rate of interest. It is almost certain that the consequence will be to add fuel to an inflationary boom if one is already under way. The fact that a low rate of interest will not necessarily induce an increase in investment in conditions of depressed demand does not mean that it will not encourage excessive demand in a period of full employment. Why, then, did not the low rate of interest provoke a much greater inflation during the war? The answer is to be found, in part, in the physical controls that had been introduced during the war; these severely curtailed the natural consequences of a low interest rate. For the rest, the answer may be summed up as better techniques of monetary manipulation by the authorities and a general sentiment that three per cent was about the right rate in the circumstances. The brilliant achievements of wartime financing under the leadership of J. M. Keynes were, however, to leave behind the illusion that what could be achieved in wartime could also be equally well achieved in peace. Post-war Chancellors of the Exchequer were to find that their task was every bit as difficult, from exactly the opposite point of view, as the task which faced their pre-war predecessors.

CHAPTER 3

American Wage Policy in Wartime

The essential difference between British and American wage policy in wartime was the same as that which distinguishes the system of industrial relations in the two countries in peacetime.

In Britain greater reliance is placed on voluntariness, the gentleman's agreement and the minimum of legal intervention, whereas in America competition is so aggressive, economic opportunism so deeply engrained, that restraint and responsibility, to be made effective, require the specific support of the law. When legal control is confined to the margins of industrial relations, public policy operates by way of broad principle; when legal control shapes and determines every manifestation of industrial relations, public policy must be clarified by code and case law. Wage policy in America had, therefore, to be worked out in far greater detail, and to be administered by much more cumbersome and complicated institutional arrangements than were necessary in Britain.

The Government in Britain, however, in one respect went very much further in limiting the freedom of the individual in relation to his employment than was the case in the United States. The extension of conscription from the military to the industrial field in Britain had no counterpart in America. It seems curious from this side of the Atlantic that the American public was prepared to accept the most far-reaching interference with the right to fix wages and yet bitterly resisted the idea of conscription. Yet it is no more curious than the British willingness to accept industrial conscription, whilst refusing adamantly to have any form of wage control. In comparing the success or failure to solve the common problem of inflation in different countries, the limitations imposed by political *mores* must be constantly kept in mind.

The establishment of a National War Labour Board by President Roosevelt in January 1942 echoed the establishment of a National War Labour Board by President Wilson in the first World War. In this respect the Americans behaved very much like the British Government, which, in substituting arbitration as a matter of legal necessity in the last resort instead of strikes or lockouts, followed a pattern which had been established in the first World War.

The National War Labour Board had been preceded by a National Defense Mediation Board which was established in March 1941, as a tripartite agency, to settle disputes referred to it by the Secretary of Labour, after all other methods of securing a peaceful settlement had been tried and failed. The Board had no power to compel a solution in cases referred, since no legal penalties were specified should the parties refuse to accept its findings. The Government could, however, in cases of non-compliance, bring pressure to bear through the threat of cancelling Government contracts and in certain instances by the seizure of plant. In practice the Board seems to have tried to behave as a mediator rather than an arbitrator, but it appears to have been compelled by the intransigence of the parties to make recommendations on many occasions.

In approximately fifteen per cent of the cases settled by the Board, one or the other of the parties refused to accept the recommendations. The personality involved in the most significant of these cases was the remarkable Mr John L. Lewis, the tough, aggressive, power-intoxicated leader of the United Mine Workers of America. The issue was one concerning the union shop in mines owned by the American steel industry. The Defense Mediation Board refused to recommend in favour of the union's claim, but the Miners would not accept this decision.[1] The CIO representatives on the Board resigned in support of the Miners and President Roosevelt found it politically convenient to sacrifice the standing of the Board, which had voted by nine to two against the Miners' claim, by devious expedients which conceded victory to John L. Lewis.

Shortly after this political intervention, which would probably have crippled the effectiveness of the National Defense Mediation Board in the future, the United States was at war with the Axis Powers. The President called a conference of trade union and employers' representatives to consider the implementation of a no-strike policy. The outcome of the discussion was an agreement that there should be no strikes or lockouts, that disputes should be settled by peaceful means and that the President should establish a National War Labour Board to resolve disputes. The two sides were, however, acutely divided on whether the Board should be empowered to arbitrate on

[1] The British National Arbitration Tribunal was faced by the same problem. When the Conditions of Employment and National Arbitration Order was changed, in 1951, disputes concerning the employment or non-employment of particular persons were specifically excluded from the jurisdiction of the Industrial Disputes Tribunal.

the issue of the 'closed shop'. The unions were emphatic that it should, and the employers were adamant against the idea. In the event the President by-passed this issue and set up a Board with the authority to formulate its own policies and to decide its own procedures.

The National Defense Mediation Board, which was wound up in favour of the new organization, was alleged to have been a failure because it had insufficient power, because it had no well worked-out policy, and because it was not staffed to undertake the responsibility of administering a fully-fledged scheme of wage control. The National War Labour Board had, with the President's support, been given authority to remedy the deficiencies of the National Defense Mediation Board and the opportunity was quickly taken to make it a most powerful wartime social institution.

Soon after the establishment of the National War Labour Board Congress passed an Emergency Price Control Act which, *inter alia*, called upon agencies of the Government to work towards a stabilization of costs of production and prices. The National War Labour Board had not, however, been given power to administer a national wages policy; its jurisdiction was limited to cases of dispute that either threatened a stoppage or were referred to it by the Federal conciliation service. There was nothing to prevent unions and employers arriving at a voluntary agreement to raise wages, nor to prevent the employer from passing on the increase in costs to the consumer in the form of higher prices.

The immediate problem which confronted the National War Labour Board was very similar to that which existed in Britain in the early months of the war. Wages were rising, not only as a result of trade union pressure, but also because employers were bidding to obtain the labour they required in an increasingly tight labour market.

Impelled by the threat of rising inflationary pressure the President sought to relieve the situation by a seven-point anti-inflation programme, under which he called for a halt to further wage increases, except to correct unfair relativities and to eliminate sub-standard rates. The War Labour Board was only able to comply with the President's programme insofar as it was called upon to resolve disputed claims for higher wages. In October Congress passed an Economic Stabilization Act which instructed the President to stabilize prices, wages and salaries at the level that prevailed on September 15, 1942, with a view to preventing the wage-price spiral from going any further upward. The President immediately issued an Executive Order empowering the National War Labour Board to veto all changes in wage rates, however determined, and it limited the Board

to authorizing changes only where necessary 'to convert maladjust-
ments, or inequalities, to eliminate substandards of living, to correct
gross inequities, or to aid in the effective prosecution of the war'.

The National War Labour Board had, in fact, taken a major step
towards the formulation of a basic policy of wage determination,
when, in July 1942, it had handed down its decision in the 'Little
Steel' case. The employees of the so-called Little Steel companies had
asked for wage increases amounting to one dollar a day and the
companies had resisted. After lengthy hearings, the War Labour
Board decided that a dollar a day would be incompatible with the
President's policy of stabilization, but it was agreed that wages ought
to be allowed to rise by as much as the increase in the cost of living
that had occurred between January, 1941, and the announcement of
the President's stabilization programme in May 1942. On this basis,
and according to the official cost of living index, the increase to
which the workers concerned were entitled was 15 per cent, which
amounted to 44 cents per day or rather less than half of what they had
demanded. The principle upon which this award was made, known as
the Little Steel formula, became the foundation stone of the Board's
future wage policy, and all subsequent claims until the end of the
war were tested against the 15 per cent increase granted to the steelworkers.

It was, therefore, assumed by the Board that the cost of living
should properly be made the basic criterion on which wage policy in
wartime should be based. Thus, in this extremely significant respect,
British and American wage policy was on all fours, but it should be
noted that the American authorities refused to commit themselves to
the principle that wages should be tied to further changes in the cost
of living.[1] Indeed, there was a strong current of opinion that real
wages would have to fall.

In another respect there was a considerable degree of similarity in
the basic approach. The National War Labour Board, like the British
Government, considered a sub-standard level as a fair reason for
raising a wage rate; it did not, however, attempt a concrete definition
of sub-standard. Every workman was entitled to a wage sufficiently
high 'to maintain a standard of living compatible with health and
decency', but the Board did not find it possible to lay down a general
rule which would relate what was sub-standard to a minimum level of
expenditure on essentials. Each case referred to the Board under this

---

[1] There seem to have been few workers covered by cost of living sliding scale
agreements, in the United States, during the second World War, so that the War
Labour Board was not faced by a problem similar to the one which existed in
Britain.

heading was considered on its merits in the light of previous decisions and prevailing circumstances. Thus the issue was, in practice, decided by reference to wage standards paid to comparable labour in comparable circumstances.

It was laid down by the Board that established differentials were an essential feature of the normal structure of wage rates and that it was no part of the Board's policy to intefere with such relationships. However, the Board was prepared to adjust rates where it could be shown that a gross inequity, giving rise to manifest injustices, existed. Though the Board would make adjustments in wages for the purpose of effectively prosecuting the war, it would not do this with the specific intention of inducing manpower to flow into the defence industries, except in 'rare and unusual' cases. The number of cases in which this criterion was actually applied was a minute fraction of the total.

The reluctance of the Board to endeavour to shape the pattern of wages, so as to guide the movement of labour, stemmed from the fear that any attempt to achieve such an aim would confuse and conflict with the basic object of achieving wage stabilization. However, the Board was well aware that it could not simply freeze wages, but the adjustments it was prepared to sanction were designed to maintain harmonious industrial relations rather than to satisfy an allocation function. At first sight this policy appears strange, when the alternative method of directing labour was not feasible for political reasons. In fact, however, wages played a considerable part in the allocation of labour to plants engaged on defence contracts. It was possible for employers to pay more to obtain the labour that they required in a variety of ways that were not illegal under the Board's regulations. Perhaps the simplest method was that of upgrading, but the provision of all kinds of fringe benefits also became important. Overtime and incentive bonus payments also allowed employers to put more into pay-packets. The attitude of the Board towards earnings was fundamentally the same as that displayed by Ernest Bevin. It considered that wage rates were the primary factor in the causation of price rises, and it looked upon increased earnings as desirable, since they were the measure of higher productivity. In other words, the Board was principally concerned to prevent wage costs pushing prices upwards and it was not its function to consider the demand side of the inflationary pressure generated by higher earnings.

In spite of the brake applied by the Board, wages and prices, under the pressure of both unions and employers, continued to creep upwards and a crisis in the stabilization programme occurred early in 1943. It was then that the President decided to try and check the increase in wages that was being granted by the Board to correct inequalities in rates of wages paid in comparable circumstances, since the cumulative effect of these decisions was to threaten the Government's stabilization policy. The 'hold-the-line' Order issued by the President restricted the Board to authorizing wage increases only to the amount allowed in the Little Steel formula, except in flagrant cases of sub-standard rates.

The National War Labour Board found the limitations imposed upon it by the President's urgent order unduly restrictive and it sought to get round the problem by adopting a new policy which would permit the Board to adjust wage rates on the basis of fair relativity within the framework of the 15 per cent maximum set by the Little Steel formula. The device invented by the Board was to establish wage rate brackets, embracing all the various 'sound and tested' rates for different occupational groups and in different wage rate areas. It was then possible for the Board to adjust particular wage rates within this stabilized system of wage brackets as and when required by the pressures of unions and employers.

The Board attempted to control the more obvious manifestations of market influence, but, even after the President's injunction to hold the line on wage rates, one of the public members has given it as his opinion that it would have been possible for an employer to double the rates of lower paid workers without running foul of the Board's regulations.[1]

Organization and Structure
The National War Labour Board was composed of an equal number of representatives of unions and employers with the addition of public members drawn mainly from the academic and legal professions.

Until early in 1943 the Board operated as a central agency, but by December 1942 it was faced with a backlog of 3,500 undecided cases. In view of this situation it was decided to establish Regional Boards in thirteen centres of industry. In addition, further sub-divisions were created to handle special industries, such as Shipbuilding, West Coast Aircraft Manufacture and Trucking. The function of the National Board, under the decentralized arrangements, was to resolve the more important disputes that were referred to the Board and to hear appeals from decisions of its sub-agencies. It was the National Board's responsibility to determine major issues of principle and policy. In order to ensure that Regional Boards carried out national policy the Board appointed a national wage stabilization director

[1] Dexter M. Keezer, 'The National War Labor Board', *American Economic Review*, June 1946.

whose main responsibility was to review the actions of the sub-divisions.

In cases where the dispute between the employer and the union could not be resolved, the United States conciliation service was authorized to refer the issue to the National War Labour Board. The Board could either deal with the case itself or refer it to one of its Regional Boards or industrial panels. Following a hearing by a panel or hearings officer a report of the findings would be made to the Regional Board, which would then issue a directive; this directive was subject to review or reconsideration by the National Board on petition by the parties, or on its own initiative.

The procedure followed in cases where a voluntary agreement on changes in wages or other conditions of employment had been reached was as follows. The employer and union filed an application for approval with the wage and hour and public contracts office; this office then sent the application on to the Regional War Labour Board or appropriate industrial commission, after it had been checked on essential detail. The Regional Board could either approve, disapprove on the basis of past decisions, or, if the application raised a new principle of national importance, send it up to the National Board, which was the final arbiter.

The Board disposed of more than 20,000 disputes, 460,000 applications for wage changes, and investigated 70,000 cases of alleged violation of the wage stabilization regulations. Since every application to change a wage rate and every dispute had to be considered in the light of previous decisions, the Government's economic policy and all the factors arising out of the particular claim, a considerable amount of work was involved. It was, therefore, necessary to build up a large clerical and administrative staff.

At its peak the Board employed in Washington, and in the field, 2,613 full-time employees; in addition several thousand part-time employees were hired by the Board to serve on the various regional boards, dispute panels, and industrial commissions.

The Board divided its organization into five divisions: (1) disputes; (2) wage stabilization; (3) legal; (4) administration; (5) information.

The functions of the disputes division, which employed persons with a specialized knowledge of industrial relations, was to take charge of all cases of dispute and to see them through to a final settlement. It had the responsibility for settling strikes and lockouts when they occurred and it was charged with the task of seeing that directives from the Board were properly carried out.

The wage stabilization division was concerned with cases of wage changes that were submitted to the Board for approval. One of its main tasks was to prepare analyses of the cases for the Board and to submit recommendations to assist it to arrive at a speedy decision. The division was also responsible for collecting a considerable amount of wage and related economic data and for the preparation of general policy evaluations for the benefit of the Board.

It was the function of the legal division to supply advice to the boards on matters of law and the legal interpretation of Executive Orders, and to see that the Board's rulings were not flouted by violations of the law.

The other two divisions were concerned with staffing, administrative and clerical services; also with the supply of information as and when required to the press and radio services.

Compared with the handful of persons who served on the National Arbitration Tribunal, the administration of wages policy in America occupied an array of people and an enormous amount of time and effort on the part of the trade unions and industry. Such a comparison is, however, not significant, since it is impossible to say what would have been the cost to America had the policy of establishing the National War Labour Board not been pursued. It is relevant only in so far as it demonstrates one of the consequences of a national wages policy, if the American model is followed.

Industrial Unrest

Since one of the prime objectives of the War Labour Board was to prevent industrial stoppages from hindering war production it is instructive to consider how far it was successful and to compare what occurred in America with British experience.

If the War Labour Board was simply to be judged in terms of successful strike avoidance, then the result is not very inspiring. The number of strikes, as Table 4 shows, increased quite considerably over the pre-war period. However, the duration of the stoppages was, on the average, very much shorter than in pre-war days, so that the effect in terms of man-days lost was not as bad as it would otherwise have been. When the frictions and pressures of wartime are taken into account, it may well be thought that without the Board the situation would have been much worse.

The War Labour Board was faced with its biggest challenge from the angle of its responsibility to settle disputes and also responsibility to stabilize wages, in the summer of 1943. By early 1943 the cost of living index had risen by almost twenty per cent over the average of 1941. The unions began to grow restive under the limitations of the fifteen per cent maximum allowed by the Little Steel formula, which had, by this time, been exhausted by most unions. The Government

TABLE 4

	Number of Strikes	Index 1935–39=100	Man-days lost (000)	Index 1935–39=100
1919	3,630	127		
1920	3,411	119		
1921	2,385	83		
1922	1,112	39		
1923	1,553	54		
1924	1,249	44		
1925	1,301	45		
1926	1,035	36		
1927	707	25	26,200	155
1928	604	21	12,600	75
1929	921	32	5,350	32
1930	637	22	3,320	20
1931	810	28	6,890	41
1932	841	29	10,500	62
1933	1,695	59	16,900	100
1934	1,856	65	19,600	116
1935	2,014	70	15,500	91
1936	2,172	76	13,900	82
1937	4,740	166	28,400	168
1938	2,772	97	9,150	54
1939	2,613	91	17,800	105
1940	2,508	81	6,700	40
1941	4,288	150	23,000	136
1942	2,968	104	4,180	25
1943	3,752	131	13,800	80
1944	4,956	173	8,720	51
1945	4,750	166	38,000	224

Source: *Bureau of Labour Statistics*

refused to relax its wage policy and sought instead to push back the rising tide of price increases. It will be seen from Table 5 that the Government failed to achieve this result, but it did succeed in holding prices remarkably steady for the next two years. This was not, however, enough to satisfy the unions, who in any case did not believe the cost of living index fairly measured the rise in prices that had actually taken place. There was a sharp increase in the number of stoppages, but many of them were 'unofficial' and none of the major unions, with one exception, showed any desire to remedy the situation by adopting a strike policy. The exception was the United Mine Workers, led by John L. Lewis.

In April 1943 Lewis launched a claim for an increase in wages of $2 per day, and he let it be known that he would accept no compromise. When the War Labour Board sought to resolve the deadlock, Lewis viciously attacked its authority and refused to attend its hearings. He stated disingenuously that he would not call a strike in wartime, but that miners would not trespass on the property of the owners in absence of a contract. Within a matter of days the miners had understood their cue and the nation faced a coal stoppage for the second time since 1941. The President at once ordered that the mines should be seized, and he appealed to the strikers to return to work.

Lewis neatly took the edge off the President's action by announcing, a few minutes before the President broadcast his statement on the situation, a fifteen days' truce in which a new contract could be worked out. The dispute continued on the basis of guerrilla war waged by Lewis for the next six months. In the end, as a result of the direct intervention of Secretary Ickes, representing the President, a compromise was reached, which nominally did not violate the Little Steel formula, but in fact gave Lewis seventy-five per cent of his demands. Not content with breaking through the wage stabilization policy Lewis rubbed in his contempt for the coal operators, the War Labour Board, the President and the public by ostentatiously refraining from ordering the miners back to work until the agreement had actually been signed.

The American Congress was not prepared to overlook Lewis's challenge; it reacted by passing a bill which, among other things, gave the War Labour Board statutory power to enforce its authority. The Unions, though by no means sympathizers of Lewis, bitterly denounced the Bill and the President vetoed it. The Congress finally had its revenge in 1947 when it carried the Taft-Hartley Act over the veto of President Truman.

The effect of Lewis's victory on the conduct of wage-stabilization was to compel the War Labour Board to adopt a relatively easy-going attitude towards fringe benefits. The Board allowed improvements in holidays with pay, allowances for travel time and lunch periods, in-

TABLE 5

	Average Weekly Earnings 1947–49 = 100	Consumer Price Index
1939	45.1	59.4
1940	47.6	59.9
1941	55.9	62.9
1942	69.2	69.7
1943	81.5	74.0
1944	87.0	75.2
1945	83.8	76.9
1946	82.8	83.4
1947	94.4	95.4
1948	102.2	102.8
1949	103.7	101.8

Source: *Bureau of Labour Statistics*

D

centive bonus and shift premiums; and it held that health and insurance benefits provided as a result of collective bargaining were outside the Board's purview.

Whilst all these concessions could be and were defended by the
War Labour Board as a necessary price of its continuance on a
tripartite basis, it could not be denied that the limitations of its power
had been exposed. In the last resort the Board depended upon con-
sent and not on coercion; it may have settled many disputes and
slowed down the pace of wage advances more successfully than would
have been the case had there been no Board, but it could no more
indefinitely dam the mighty economic pressures generated by the war,
than the barrage at Aswan could indefinitely hold up the waters of
the Nile. A flood could be held back only by allowing a steady release
through the sluice gates.

Wage Stabilization and Prices
It was never the intention of the American Government to stabilize
wages by freezing them for the duration, but it was hoped to prevent
any general increase in wage rates for the duration of the war. Basic
wages did, in fact, rise by twenty-four per cent between January 1941
and July 1945, but two-thirds of this increase occurred before the
War Labour Board was authorized to control voluntary wage agreements. Gross weekly earnings rose, however, by seventy-one per
cent. A great proportion of this increase in earnings resulted from
factors over which the War Labour Board had no control, such as
changes in the composition of the work force, increases in number of
workers on piece-rates and the amount of overtime worked. A not
inconsiderable amount of higher earnings fell within the area of control exercised by the Board, and was the result of legitimate and
illegitimate increases paid by employers.

The increases in wage rates between 1941 and 1945 were roughly
similar in Britain and America, but earnings went ahead far more
rapidly in the United States. During this period the cost of living
advanced by about thirty-three per cent in the United States and by
approximately twenty per cent in Britain. In both countries workers
made substantial gains in real wages during the war period, if actual
earnings are used as the measuring rod rather than wage rates. The
unions in both Britain and America disputed the validity of measuring
wartime gains in this way. They argued that since the high earnings
were the result of increased effort they did not represent an increase
in the share of the product of industry. Furthermore, since the wartime advances in earnings were the result of an extraordinary level of
demand generated by the war, their gains would be lost immediately

the war was over. It was, therefore, only legitimate to compare the rise in wage rates with the rise in prices, and on this basis the increase in real income had been very small.

The reasoning of the unions is understandable but it does not alter the fact that total money incomes going to wage-earners rose to a far greater extent than prices during the war. From the point of view of stabilizing prices total wages rose too much in both countries, but from the point of view of maintaining reasonably good industrial relations and adequate mobility it would almost certainly not have been possible to have kept them very much lower.

Prices were controlled by an agency, the Office of Price Stabilization, that was entirely separate from the War Labour Board. Though the Little Steel formula was based on the rise in the cost of living the notion that wages should be specifically tied to changes in prices was rejected as a principle on which wage policy should be based; and the idea that wage increases should be determined by reference to their likely effect on prices was rarely carried from the general to the specific. From May 1943 no wage change which entailed a rise in a price ceiling could be allowed by the War Labour Board without the approval of the Director of Economic Stabilization, but changes were, in fact, virtually never disapproved on these grounds.[1]

Price control would have been far more difficult to administer had the full pressure of the increase in money incomes been felt. High taxation, a substantial increase in savings and a moderate but not insignificant increase in consumer goods, did a great deal to keep the inflation within bounds. At the same time as American industry was churning out the essentials of war, it was also able to increase the output of goods for civilian use by something approaching twenty per cent, thus enabling real consumption to rise by this amount.

Rationing and subsidies, in these circumstances, never assumed the some degree of importance to the American authorities, as a means of helping to stabilize prices, as they did to the British. Strategic raw materials and key items of manufacture were controlled to some degree; certain industries were starved of their supplies for civilian use and had to close down, or reduce their operations; and subsidies were paid in particular cases to help the Administration to achieve its aims. The colossal reserve of productivity which resulted in a flow of the instruments of war that astonished the world, made the kind of detailed controls of production and labour which were vitally required in Britain almost unnecessary in America.

[1] J. T. Dunlop, 'An Appraisal of Wage Stabilization Policies, Problems and Policies of Dispute Settlement and Wage Stabilization During World War II', *BLS Bulletin*, No. 1,009, 1950.

The very success, however, which the American authorities achieved in suppressing the inflationary pressure by wage and price controls banked up pressures which, when released by the end of the war, created a tremendous problem. As controls were relaxed, prices at once began to rise. Wage increases were permitted, in theory, so long as they had no effect on prices, but the President's appeal to both labour and employers not to abandon restraint rang hollow when the fighting had ceased. The War Labour Board was wound up and a Wage Stabilization Board set up in its place. This was no more than a gesture to the desirability of a smooth return to full collective bargaining. A great dispute began at once as to the extent to which industry could pay wage increases out of 'swollen profits' without raising prices. Both sides were bent on having a test of strength. The employers felt that the unions had grown too powerful during the war, and the unions were fearful that the employers would stop at nothing to weaken their bargaining strength. In the twelve months that followed V-J Day 4,630 stoppages involving more than five million workers and a loss of 120 million working days had occurred. But in spite of these setbacks the American economy settled down to a top-gear performance and the driving mechanism, by comparison with the inter-war period, has run for more than a decade with an efficiency that few at the end of the war would have dreamed possible. A vitally important feature of the post-war situation has been the development of a mature collective bargaining relationship between the unions and employers. This was only possible on a basis of mutual respect, which came when both sides decided that it was futile to try to make radical changes in the pattern which had emerged at the end of the war. Out of this situation there has developed a whole range of wage and income security policies which have posed new economic problems. These new policies were just emerging when the American economy was once again threatened with disruption by the outbreak of war in Korea. How the Government sought to cope with that situation and the way in which the unions and employers responded will be discussed in a later chapter.

CHAPTER 4

Wage Policy under the Labour Government

The problem of maintaining full employment in the future became a major political issue during the second World War; discussion centred mainly on the methods that might be employed to secure a sufficiency of expenditure that would achieve jobs for all, but the need to avoid inflation as an inevitable accompaniment of full employment was recognized as a factor of vital significance.

The difficulties that would be posed by the abolition of unemployment in a peacetime economy were succinctly expressed in a powerful article by a special correspondent which appeared in *The Times* on January 23, 1943.

'Unemployment in a private-enterprise economy has not only the function of preserving discipline in industry, but also indirectly the function of preserving the value of money. If free wage-bargaining, as we have known it hitherto, is continued in conditions of full employment, there would be a constant upward pressure upon money wage-rates. This phenomenon also exists at the present time, and is also kept within bounds by the appeal of patriotism. In peacetime the vicious spiral of wages and prices might become chronic. This would bring a variety of evils in its train. It would greatly complicate the problem of controlling international trade, since it would require offsetting movements in exchange rates. It would bring about an arbitrary distribution of real income within the country, rentiers, salary-earners, and ill-organized workers losing relatively to the members of the strong trade unions, who would secure the greatest wage advances, and to the industrialists, who could recoup themselves for rising costs by raising prices. Finally, if it moved too fast it might precipitate a violent inflation.'

The danger that under conditions of full employment there would be a rising spiral of wages and prices leading to inflation appeared sufficiently important for Sir William Beveridge (as he then was) to seek from the Economic Council of the TUC a statement of their attitude to this problem. He also asked the General Council to consider whether it would be possible to ensure an adequate mobility of labour in a condition of full employment.

In their reply the General Council saw 'no need to fear such a spiral if the Government can convince the Movement that in genuine pursuit of a policy of full employment it is determined to take all other steps that are necessary to control prices and can convince the Trade Union Movement of the need to secure equivalent guarantees that wage movements will not be such as to upset the system of price control'.[1]

The General Council added that, in such circumstances, it would be the duty of the Trade Union Movement to give suitable guarantees about wage settlements and reasonable assurances that such guarantees would be generally observed. It was clear, however, from the Report that the General Council envisaged nothing more than a voluntary declaration by the unions that they would behave in a responsible fashion. In no circumstances would the Council accept the notion that workmen should be compelled to accept terms and conditions of employment. The General Council, it is clear from the Report, was far more concerned about the achievement of full employment than about the difficulties that might ensue. The danger of inflation was dismissed as mainly a problem of the immediate post-war period. 'Once the transition period has passed, the danger of inflation even under a condition of full employment can easily be exaggerated. Minor fluctuations in demand can usually be absorbed by drawing upon stocks. Moreover, there are always reserves of productive capacity and labour which can easily be tapped under full employment.'[2]

In the Coalition Government's White Paper on Full Employment, presented by the Minister of Reconstruction to Parliament in May 1944, the stability of wages and prices was stated to be a 'condition vital to the success of employment policy'. The Government would be prepared to do what it could to stabilize prices, but both sides of industry would have to co-operate to keep costs down and they would have to take steps to prevent restrictive practices and agreements from forcing up prices. The failure of workers to move to places and occupations where they were needed could also frustrate the policy of the Government and lead to a dangerous rise in prices. If, therefore, an expansion in total expenditure was not to lead to inflation, there would have to be adequate mobility of labour.

Continuance of National Arbitration Order
Although the General Council had stated in its Report on Post-War

[1] TUC *Annual Report*, 1944, Appendix D.
[2] *Ibid.*

Reconstruction that it would not in any circumstances invite the State to impose a system of compulsory arbitration, it agreed with the Government and with the employers' organizations that it would be wise to continue the wartime regulations which made strikes illegal and provided facilities for arbitration instead. The agreement to continue the Order was subject to the provision that both the employers and the unions would be free to recommend its abolition at any time they should feel this step desirable. The readiness of the trade unions to accept the continuation of regulations which made strikes illegal was due to their anxiety to secure a smooth transition from a wartime to a peacetime economy, rather than to fear of inflation. They had no desire to see strikes embarrass the Labour Government in its efforts to grapple with the problems of reconstruction.

A Tentative Approach to Wage Policy
The continuance of the National Arbitration Order and other wartime regulations was undoubtedly a wiser policy than indulging in an incontinent rush to freedom, but since, even during the war, it had proved impossible to stabilize prices, in spite of controls and appeals to the patriotism of the unions, there could be no certainty that the task would prove possible in peacetime.

That there would be an immediate pressure for wage increases as soon as the war was over was only to be expected. Most trade unionists were afraid that they would lose their wartime gains if they could not quickly consolidate them in higher wage rates; some were deeply concerned at changes in their relative wage position and were bent on restoring traditional relationships; others simply felt the urge to exploit the end of the war. In these circumstances it was inevitable that wage increases would occur, and they could be looked upon as a necessary post-war readjustment.

It soon became obvious, however, that the pressure for wage increases would seriously endanger the reconstruction programme, unless a brake could be applied and productivity be accelerated. In January 1947 a 'Statement on the Economic Considerations affecting relations between Employers and Workers' was issued by the Government with the full support of the National Joint Advisory Council. This document stressed the vital necessity of increasing output, of moving labour into the under-manned export and basic industries, of keeping costs and prices steady. As a statement of policy it was, unfortunately, a failure, since no indication was given of the measures that were required to achieve the objectives set forth. Every hint of resolution had been emasculated by the need to secure agreement; in these circumstances the document aroused neither strong opposition nor great enthusiasm, and it had little effect on the course of events.

The unusually severe winter and the acute fuel crisis engendered by the great blizzard, which brought transport almost to a standstill, dramatically exposed the brink of disaster on which the fortunes of the nation teetered. Workers had to be recruited by the essential industries in one way or another. The miners naturally advocated higher wages as the solution to attracting more labour, but Arthur Deakin, General Secretary of the Transport Workers' Union, in his emphatic, strident manner denounced the idea of a Government-inspired wage policy as an intolerable invasion of trade union rights. He indicated that he would be prepared to accept the direction of labour rather than agree to his members being paid at rates the alteration of which the unions were not free to seek.

The Government, stimulated by the convertability crisis of 1947, eventually screwed up its courage to go beyond exhortation and, with the support of the unions, introduced a Control of Engagements Order which took effect in October 1947. Workers covered by the Order were compelled to use the Labour Exchanges when changing employment and could be directed to essential jobs. More significantly, the Minister of Labour drew the attention of both sides of a number of joint negotiating bodies to an appeal by the Prime Minister for restraint in wage demands, especially where they were based on the maintenance of differentials. The unions immediately protested and the Prime Minister quickly promised not to interfere in this fashion again, but the dangers of the situation were put to the unions, who were asked to consider what should be done. All that emerged from the discussions was another polite suggestion that restraint should be exercised. This rather pathetic appeal to reason had no more effect on the behaviour of the unions than a whispered 'whoa' to a deaf cart-horse, which, blinkered by tradition, could not see that the road bent and that if it kept straight on it would drag the economy off the hard surface into an inflationary morass.

A Bolder Attack on the Problem
Afraid that unless something more drastic was done economic disaster would engulf the nation and would wreck its social reforms the Labour Government suddenly issued, without consultation, a statement on Personal Incomes, Costs and Prices.[1] This document followed the now familiar presentation of the dangers of inflation with a blunt statement that there should be no further increases in the level of personal incomes except on the basis of a corresponding

[1] Cmd. 7321, HMSO 1948.

increase in production. It re-emphasized a point made previously by
the Prime Minister, that the attempt to maintain traditional differentials was flying in the face of modern industrial needs. Relative incomes must be adjusted so as to bring about the movement of labour
and resources into those industries where they were most required.

For the benefit of those responsible for determining the level
of personal income it laid down four general principles: (1) that the
Government should not seek directly to control the incomes of
individuals except by taxation; (2) that both parties should not depart
from the terms of collective agreements, since this would lead to
competitive bargaining; (3) that there was no justification for any
general increase in money incomes, since this would merely add to
costs and so raise prices; (4) that in spite of the danger of inflation it
would not be right to freeze all wages at their current levels, since
increases in wages and salaries would be justified from a national point
of view where that was necessary in order to attract labour to under-
manned industries. It was also admitted that any marked rise in the
cost of living would be grounds for reconsidering those incomes which
were, as a result, rendered inadequate. Only if these principles were
followed could the Government avoid the undesirable necessity of
interfering with the established methods of free negotiation. This
threat was reinforced by a warning to employers that the Government
would not henceforth be bound to take into account an increase in
wage costs when fixing controlled price levels.

The General Council of the TUC once again protested at not
being consulted, but in view of the meagre results that had been
achieved from the discussions in the previous few months the protest
rang rather hollow. There was, however, substance in their argument
that they would have difficulty in persuading their members to accept
the Government's proposals. The White Paper scarcely mentioned
profits, and the Chancellor of the Exchequer sought to meet the
unions' criticisms that employers' incomes were being treated less
vigorously than workers' incomes, by linking the call for wage and
salary restraint with a similar call for voluntary dividend limitation.

The General Council of the TUC were now persuaded that the
economic situation was sufficiently desperate to warrant the acceptance of the Government's policy, with reservations. The Council was
not prepared to agree to the abolition of those established differentials that were required to sustain craftsmanship, or to refrain from
pressing for adjustments in the wages of workers whose incomes
were below 'a reasonable standard of subsistence'. It also insisted
that increased output must be grounds for increasing wages. Thus, it
would not be difficult, in practice, for any union to find one reason or

another to justify a wage claim, but in spite of this the General Council was genuinely anxious to co-operate with the Government. Though the Council's recommendations were accepted by 5,421,000 votes to 2,032,000, the large minority against approval demonstrated the limitations of the Council's authority over the affiliated unions.

The adoption of the Personal Incomes, Costs and Prices policy was a triumph for the Labour Prime Minister, Mr Attlee, and his Chancellor of the Exchequer, Sir Stafford Cripps. No Government in either peace or war had, in modern times, attempted to brake and steer the movement of wages so precisely as was now proposed. But would the trade union movement and employers' organizations, which had in principle agreed to co-operate, be able to fulfil, in practice, the spirit of the policy they had endorsed?

As will be seen from the graph on page 65, wage rates were not frozen during the next two years and earnings continued to rise. The trading profit of companies, having risen substantially in 1947, increased only slightly in 1948 and actually fell in 1949, but recovered in 1950. Distributed dividends and interest were cut back in 1948 and 1949 from the high figure reached in 1947, but were substantially raised in 1950.

The inflation was checked to the extent of allowing the gold and dollar reserves to recover from the pitiable figure of £457 million, to which they had fallen in 1948, to £603 million in 1949.[1] But there was little, if any, reduction in the total supply of money, since the Government was unable to reduce its own borrowing.[2] Net bank deposits and notes in circulation continued to rise[3] as capital investment and consumers' expenditure went up.[4] Under the pressure of consumer demand and rising costs retail prices could not be held down,[5] although production was rising at a far from derisory rate. To make matters worse, a slight recession in America which began in the spring of 1949, cut dollar earnings from sterling area products to less than half; later a run on sterling threatened to deplete the quite inadequate reserves.

It was against this background of circumstances that the Government decided on the bold course of devaluing the pound by forty per cent, in a once-and-for-all attempt to improve Britain's balance of payments difficulties. This decision underlined the extreme seriousness of the economic situation and dramatically pointed up the sig-

[1] LCES *Bulletin*, Table 11.
[2] *Ibid.*, Tables 21 and 22.
[3] *Ibid.*, Tables 13 and 14.
[4] *Ibid.*, Table 88
[5] *Ibid.*, Table 1.

nificance of wage restraint; it was, however, also a confession of the failure of that policy. The facts of the situation dictated that real incomes should be cut if the balance of payments was to become sufficiently favourable to restore the gold and dollar reserves to a respectable figure. Sir Stafford Cripps's magnificently austere appeal for self-denial met with a superficially favourable response; everybody felt that they were virtuously practising austerity whilst continuing to behave exactly as they had been doing. The economic crisis evoked the same kind of self-deception as to the dangers of the situation that prevailed after Dunkirk, when Hitler's invasion was never quite taken seriously. Austerity became a national joke that was doubly enjoyable because it was something to grumble about and because real incomes, if not rising rapidly, were certainly not falling.

By the beginning of 1950 there were already clear indications that the wage restraint policy was breaking down. The unions adopted the simple but disingenuous device of voting at the TUC in favour of wage restraint whilst at the same time seeking 'justifiable' wage increases.

The devaluation of the pound was bound to bring wage restraint to an end, since it necessarily involved a sharp rise in import prices that could only have been offset by a substantial fall in home demand, and by a much greater rise in productivity than in fact was taking place. The General Council of the TUC recognized the consequences which the failure of the Chancellor's gamble would bring and they responded to the challenge by a courageous attempt to bind together the crumbling support for wage restraint. It was suggested by the Council that unions should not press wage claims so long as the price index did not rise by more than five points, and that those unions with cost of living sliding scales should forego their entitlement to wage increases in order to maintain stability for at least a year. An offer by the Government to establish a statutory minimum wage, an objective at one time sought by the TUC, was, however, rejected. Here then, was a bold recognition of the harsh facts of Britain's economic situation by a body that has so often been severely criticized for its myopia and timidity, and even, of irresponsibility. The wisdom of the Council was not matched by a sympathetic response from the lower levels of trade union leadership. It was only too easy for Communist-inspired propagandists with entrenched positions in certain unions to rouse hostile opinion against the temporary sacrifice which the Council was calling upon trade unionists to make in their long-term interests. When the General Council put its policy to a specially convened conference of trade union executives it was carried, but only by the narrow majority of 4,263,000 votes to

3,606,000. The signs were there for everybody to read; the policy had been carried, but would never be put into effect. The unions with sliding scales refused to sacrifice their advantages; the engineers and railwaymen continued to press their demands for wage increases, and the miners and distributive workers voted to reject the policy which had been supported by their leaders.

The General Council, faced by the obvious failure of its gallant attempt to support the Government's efforts to suppress inflation, tried to save the remnants of its policy, but the 1950 Trades Union Congress pursued the humiliation of the Council to its logical end. The resolution calling for the termination of wage restraint was carried against the opposition of the Council by only a narrow majority, but the fate of Sir Stafford Cripps's 1948 White Paper policy had been settled. The rapid increase in import prices stimulated by the Korean War made price stabilization almost impossible, and the unleashing of the unions and upsurge in demand for labour added greatly to costs. Wages, salaries and dividends per unit of output went up at a tremendous pace, in 1951 and 1952, as the following table shows:

TABLE 6

	1948	1949	1950	1951	1952	1953
Output	100	105	109	111	110	115
Wages and salaries	100	106	112	126	134	142
Wages and salaries per unit of output	100	101	103	114	122	123
Interest and dividends	100	103	107	120	125	140
Interest and dividends per unit of output	100	98	96	108	114	122

The balance of payments again began to deteriorate and the handsome net balance of £300 million realized in 1950 was turned into the frightening deficit of £403 million in 1951. With the reserves running out at a fearful pace, Mr Gaitskell, the Chancellor of the Exchequer, turned in desperation to the trade unions and offered to attack prices by limiting dividends by legal imposition, extending controls, prohibiting resale price maintenance, strengthening the monopolies commission and increasing subsidies. It may be doubted whether these efforts to curb price increases would have assuaged the unions' thirst for higher incomes; it is quite certain that had they been put into effect they would not have subdued the inflation, unless incomes had been reduced, or production had suddenly and substantially increased. As it was, these measures were never put to the test, since the Labour Party was defeated at the election which the Government had been compelled to hold by the loss of confidence in its policies. In the defeat which the Labour Government sustained, no factor played a greater part than the rise in the cost of living. The increase in prices was in part due to factors beyond the Government's control, but the problem was very greatly exaggerated by the rate at which money incomes rose. The determination of the unions to win a substantial advance in wages for their members met with a flabby resistance from employers who found no difficulty in passing on higher labour costs in higher prices. As the cost of living rose it soured the success of the unions and stimulated them to make further demands, but every effort to offset price increases by wage increases was to large extent doomed to inevitable frustration. In circumstances in which the cost of imports had risen by twenty per cent and British export prices were not below competitive levels, it was impossible for the unions to improve the real wages of their members by raising money wages, except in so far as other incomes could be held stable or reduced. There was a certain amount of redistribution, but more could only have been achieved at the price of lowering incentives, encouraging a black market and probably inducing a flight of capital and the emigration of large numbers of the technical, professional and business classes.

In the situation which faced the Labour Government in the post-war period important elements were not susceptible to its manipulation; others were determined at a prior level of policy making. The scale of expenditure on arms flowed from the state of world affairs rather than from a calculation of what the nation could afford. Exports had to be vastly increased, not only to pay for a massive increase in imports, but also to pay off the huge total of incurred debts and to assist backward territories. These basic demands on resources would have presented any Government with an inescapable load; they were not, therefore, as is sometimes suggested, the cause of the inflationary problems. The fundamental task of the Government was to see that all other claims did not exceed the residue of available resources.

It is now generally recognized that the monetary policy of the Labour Government was not the most suitable from the point of view of restraining inflationary demands on the limited supply of resources. Whatever might be said for and against using the rate of interest as an economic regulator, it can, at any rate, be asserted with absolute confidence, that a policy of cheap money, as pursued by the Labour Party, will not do anything to stop an inflation. Moreover, the effort to keep the rate of interest low is likely to lead the Government to issue a large volume of Treasury Bills, which then form the basis of a credit expansion by the banks. Thus the demand for Government bonds will be kept up and the rate of interest will remain low, but the increase in the supply of money and the low interest rates, will stimulate borrowing for purposes of investment and consumption. A cheap money policy will, therefore, increase the demand for goods and services at the very time when monetary policy ought to be having exactly the opposite effect.

Since the war had been financed at three per cent, Dr Dalton could be forgiven for desiring to finance the peace at two-and-a-half per cent. The low rate of interest during the war was, however, bolstered by a high level of savings, by a patriotic willingness to accept abstention as a duty, as well as by physical controls. When the Labour Government pinned its faith in the continued effectiveness of these policies it failed to appreciate that the responses evoked by war might not be as strong in peacetime. The electorate, in 1945, gave the Labour Party a mandate to reconstruct the economic and social life of the nation on more egalitarian lines than hitherto, but a vote for the welfare state was not a vote pledging the abandonment of self-interest. If inflation was to be prevented it would have to be with and not against the self-interest of the most powerful groups in the community.

Of all the pressure groups to which the Labour Government might be vulnerable the trade unions were the most powerful and most awkward to deal with. They were organically linked to the Labour Party by affiliation; they were the main source of the Party's funds; they were strongly represented in the House of Commons and in the Government. No Government would have been in a position to ignore the unions after the war, but a Labour Government was subject to internal as well as external pressures. To some extent the very closeness of the Labour Government to the unions placed it in a position where it could appeal directly to the members of the unions. The leaders of the unions often bitterly complained that members of the Government thought that they knew as well as union officials what was good for the workers. Whenever the Government by-passed the unions, as in 1948, when a letter was sent by the Minister of Labour to Wages Boards and Wages Councils, calling attention to the contents of the White Paper on Personal Incomes, Costs and Prices, the union leaders vigorously protested. During each of the three Labour Governments the trade unions have made it plain through the TUC that they would not be bound by any policy simply because it emerged from a Labour Government. The unions at all times should be free to decide their own policy, to decide whether to co-operate with the Government or not; free to oppose, if necessary, with every weapon at their disposal, any policy which they felt might harm their fundamental interests.

Here, then, was the dilemma which faced the Labour Government;

on the basis of its general economic policy it could only prevent inflation by holding wages down; it could only raise productivity quickly by ensuring that under-manned industries obtained adequate supplies of labour. These objectives could be reached (1) by administrative controls, which fixed maximum wages and made certain that they were not exceeded, and by the direction of labour; (2) by voluntary wage restraint that was really made effective by the unions and employers, and by a union and employer wage policy that adjusted differentials so as to secure the voluntary mobility of labour; or (3) by the pursuit of a sufficiently disinflationary policy by the Government which would, by curtailing the supply of money, prevent wages from rising, and, by creating some unemployment, make possible the urgently needed transference of labour to the under-manned industries. Unfortunately for the Labour Government, the unions were not prepared to accept any of these alternative policies.

The problem which faced the unions must also be seen. They could only accept the planned socialist solution, involving detailed controls, if they abandoned free collective bargaining and became, as had the Russian trade unions, an administrative agency of the state. This, they knew, would be fatal to the traditional conceptions of free trade unionism and would not be accepted by union members. Such a solution, it was felt, was only possible in a totalitarian state. Though it had been possible in wartime to conscript and direct labour to wherever it was required, in peacetime direction, even when accepted in preference to a national wage policy, proved to be abortive. It was a failure because the Ministry of Labour dared not use the powers at its command.[1] The net result was that the much vaunted manpower planning of the Labour Government was reduced to a farce; the targets were missed by such huge margins that their continued publication became an acute source of embarrassment and they were discontinued.[2]

Voluntary wage restraint might be regarded as a success insofar as the rate of wage increase was slowed down for two years. It was not, however, slowed down sufficiently to permit the stabilization of prices and the building up of substantial gold and dollar reserves.

[1] In the first two years of the operation of the Control of Engagements Order only 600 directions were issued; 400 of these were orders refusing transference from the coal industry; only twenty-nine people were directed to industries other than coal and agriculture.

[2] For an excellent discussion of the Labour Government's manpower policy and problems encountered see S. E. Rolfe, 'Manpower Allocation under British Planning', *American Economic Review*, June 1954; and 'Trade Unions, Freedom, and Economic Planning', *Proceedings*, Industrial Relations Research Association (1950).

Wage restraint failed because the unions were unable to resist the temptation to press for higher wages. It would hardly be fair, however, to blame the unions for carrying out the wishes of their members. Since it was apparent that employers were willing to pay more to obtain the labour that they required, and since some unions were quite willing to exploit this situation, even if the rest had been paragons of virtue they would probably have given way to such seductive encouragement. So long as the demand for labour exceeded the supply, and employers could pass on increased costs in one way or another, there was no barrier to wage increases, and no union could stand aside for long in these circumstances without endangering its viability as an institution.

If it had been possible for the trade union movement to act as a single organization and for the employers to have done likewise, so that a comprehensive wage policy could have been worked out and enforced, then it might have been possible to control the movement of wages. This idea, though canvassed at the TUC and in articles, never had the remotest possibility of acceptance.[1] In the first instance too large a proportion of wage and salary earners were unorganized, as were a large number of employers. Secondly, the central bodies in both cases had no power to compel their constituents to accept, let alone carry out, a national wages policy. This kind of self-administered wage policy has been tried by the unions and employers in Sweden and it will be examined in Chapter 6.

Since the third alternative open to the Government, that of a resolute disinflationary economic policy, was ruled out by its desire to maintain a state of brimful employment, it could only fall back on a series of makeshift, hope-for-the-best expedients. Whilst it is easy to criticize the Labour Government for failing to face the challenge, it is also difficult to see what else they could have done in the circumstances, given their objectives and in face of the power of the trade unions.

Even more open to criticism, however, were the trade unions. The leaders of the Party saw the dilemma and wanted to do something about it; as witness the acceptance by Hugh Dalton on behalf of the Executive of a resolution in favour of a national wages policy, at the 1947 Party Conference, and the Labour Party Pamphlet, *Fair Shares for All*. The unions, however, wanted absolutely full employment, cheap money, massive government expenditures, stable prices, and freedom to bargain for higher wages as and when they liked, without any limits. Experience during the period in which the Labour Gov-

---

[1] All the problems likely to arise from this proposal were discussed by H. W. Singer, 'Wages Policy in Full Employment', *Economic Journal*, December 1947.

WEEKLY WAGE RATES, WEEKLY EARNINGS, & RETAIL PRICES
(RATIO SCALE)

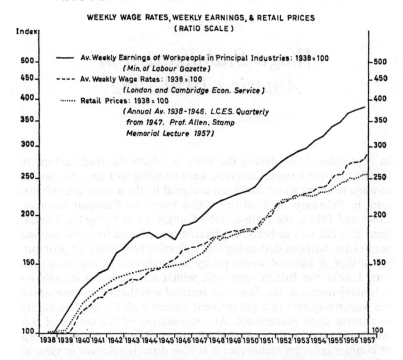

ernment was in office showed that these objectives were mutually incompatible. Perhaps in a subconscious way the electorate realized that the dilemmas could not be solved without a change of government. At any rate, in voting for a Conservative Government in 1951, the electorate recorded a verdict of no confidence in the Labour Party's handling of the economic situation. The Conservatives were pledged to 'set the people free' from controls and to tackle the problem of inflation by more orthodox monetary and fiscal policies. Before examining their record we must now turn to some other attempts in countries overseas to deal with the fundamental economic problem of our time.

E

CHAPTER 5

Wage Stabilization in America 1950-1952

In September 1950, during the week in which the trade unions in Britain, at their annual Congress, were bringing to a close the period of wage restraint which had been accepted by them since the publication, in February 1948, of the White Paper on Personal Incomes, Costs and Prices, the United States Congress was laying the foundations of what was to become a fascinating attempt to work out and administer, without destroying free collective bargaining or prohibiting strikes, a national wages policy in conditions of less than total war. Unlike the British approach, which rested almost entirely on voluntary restraint, the American method was that of re-establishing the wartime system of a government agency with the legal authority to control wage movements. An examination of the course of this American experiment is of particular interest from the point of view of counter-inflation technique; it is also directly relevant in view of the fact that the TUC twice summarily rejected, in 1950 and 1951, resolutions calling upon the General Council to examine the wisdom of this country pursuing a national wages policy of an almost identical type.[1]

[1] At the 1950 Trades Union Congress Mr A. L. N. D. Houghton, MP (Inland Revenue Staff Federation), moved the following resolution: 'That in the opinion of this Congress, acceptance by the Trade Union Movement of the economic planning essential for the pursuit of full employment and other social objectives increases the responsibility of trade unions for wage movements and wage structure since their influence on the price level, on the distribution of manpower, and on productivity is a matter of general concern. Congress recognizes that new problems of wages policy arise on account of full employment and economic planning, and is of opinion that the General Council should consider the setting up of a National Wages Board constituted on the lines of the Industrial Court with an independent chairman and independent members and other members drawn equally from workers' and employers' panels. The General Council is therefore asked to examine and report upon the proposal to set up a National Wages Board with the following functions:
(a) the supervision and approval of the decisions of all statutory wage-fixing bodies (Wages Councils, etc.).
(b) the supervision and approval of all voluntary collective agreements relating to terms of employment, which would have to be registered with the board;

Under the powers conferred upon him by the Defence Production Act,[1] the President of the United States proclaimed a national emergency on December 16, 1950, and announced the establishment of an Office of Defence Mobilization, with Charles E. Wilson, President of the General Electric Corporation, as Director. This office was given power 'to direct, control and co-ordinate all mobilization activities of the Executive Branch of the Government including but not limited to production, procurement, manpower, stabilization and transport activities'. Several new agencies were set up to carry the Administration's programme into effect. Mr Eric Johnston, well known for his negotiations on behalf of the American film industry, was appointed Administrator of an Economic Stabilization Agency with two subdivisions, the Office of Price Stabilization and the Wage Stabilization Board.[2] These two sub-agencies were charged with the task of working out and administering the detailed policies of price and wage control for the Economic Stabilization Agency. Although the decisions of the Wage Stabilization Board were, in effect, decisions of the Economic Stabilization Agency, the board had a good deal of independent authority, though its actions were influenced by the wider policy of economic stabilization which the Government had been authorized by Congress to pursue.

The Wage Stabilization Board was established on a tripartite basis, its nine members being appointed to represent the trade unions, industry, and the public—three from each—with Mr Cyrus S. Ching, head of the Federal Conciliation and Mediation Service, as Chairman. On January 26, 1951, the Economic Stabilization Administrator issued an order establishing ceilings on the prices of materials and services, and, following the provisions of the Defence Production Act, which required that upon the issue of such an order wages and salaries must also be stabilized, a general regulation was made freezing all wages and salaries at levels not greater than those prevailing on the previous day until such time as the Wage Stabilization Board authorized an increase.[3] This step was not regarded as

(c) the co-ordination of the work of all arbitration tribunals, acting itself as the supreme arbitration authority;
(d) the initiation of inquiries with a view to recommending reforms in existing wage structures.'

[1] Public Law 774, 81st Congress, September 8, 1950.
[2] On May 10th a separate Salary Stabilization Board was set up, composed of five public members, with the chairman of the Wage Stabilization Board as an ex-officio member. In the exercise of its functions the board must 'conform to the regulations, policies, orders, and decisions of the Wage Stabilization Board to the fullest practicable extent . . .'. General Order No. 8, Economic Stabilization Agency.
[3] General Wage Stabilization Regulation No. 1.

more than a temporary expedient until the Wage Stabilization Board had developed a policy for the future. Within a few days the Board made its first important decision when it permitted the United Mineworkers to have the benefit of an increase in wages which had been negotiated, but had not yet been put into effect prior to the regulation. This decision seemed ominous to many people, for John L. Lewis had, with his usual facility, sensed that the wages stop was coming and had seized the opportunity to secure a substantial advance for the miners; and now the barrier to wage increases which had come down was being lifted slightly to allow them to enjoy it. However, to have provoked a miners' strike would not have been an auspicious start for the Board.

During the few weeks following the wage freeze the Board tried unsuccessfully to arrive at an agreed policy. The problem immediately confronting it was that the freeze had created considerable inequities between industries, as any wage freeze is bound to do. In 1949 wage rates had remained practically stable, but a number of unions had followed the pattern set by the Mineworkers and United Automobile Workers and had secured, instead of wage increases, pension, health, and welfare benefits, paid for in whole or in part by the companies. Although money wages had not risen much during 1949 prices had fallen slightly, so that real wages had increased by a trifle; this trend, however, was reversed in 1950 when prices began to rise. From shortly before the outbreak of the Korean War until August the pace of the climb upwards was rapid, then it slackened until November, when a swift acceleration again began which continued until the end of January 1951, when the price and wage stabilization orders were made.[1]

[1] *Consumers' Price Index.* The monthly average of this index was 171.9, 1949, 170.2 (1935–39=100). In the course of 1950 the Index moved as follows:

1950	January 15th	168.2
	February 15th	167.9
	March 15th	167.4
	April 15th	168.5
	May 15th	169.3
	June 15th	170.2
	July 15th	172.5
	August 15th	173.0
	September 15th	174.6
	October 15th	175.6
	November 15	176.4
	December 15th	178.8
1951	January 15th	181.5
	February 15th	183.8

Source: Bureau of Labour Statistics, *Monthly Labour Review*

At the beginning of 1950 unions were willing to accept contracts which gave them only a few cents an hour increase, but by the end of the year, partly as a consequence of the rise in the cost of living and partly because wage controls were feared, agreements were being made which gave increases of 10, 15, and 20 cents an hour. Many employers were ready to agree to substantial increases in order to be certain of securing a future supply of labour. Not all industries, however, were prosperous, and not all employers were either ready or in a position to be generous—about 40 per cent of wage-earners had no increases at all in 1950. Following such a period of rapid change the wage freeze inevitably created a good deal of injustice; had the economic stabilization programme been put into operation six months earlier many of the acute problems which the Wages Board had to solve might have been avoided.

On February 16th the public and industry members of the Board adopted what was in essence the 'Little Steel formula' all over again, without the support of the trade union members, to deal with the situation which the wage freeze had created.[1] The effect of the proposal was that the Board would permit wages to rise by ten per cent, where they had not already done so, above levels being paid on a base date fixed as January 15, 1950. No application for permission to bring wage levels up to this amount above the wage base was necessary provided complete information about all such increases was filed with the Board within ten days of the increase being given effect. The Board reserved the right to revoke any increase which it considered exceeded the ten per cent limit. Where it could be established that the wage rates prevailing in an industry on the base date were abnormal the Board was ready to authorize a different base, and in cases where 'the critical needs of essential civilian or defence production require it' the Board announced that it would consider applications for increases above the ten per cent limit. In the latter instance such increases would be confined to 'rare and unusual' cases 'where there are serious manpower shortages and in which other governmental agencies concerned with production and manpower problems certify to the Board that a concerted programme has been undertaken to remedy the shortages and that an increase in wages, salaries or other compensation is indispensable to attract required labour to or retain in essential civilian or defence industries or plants'.[2] The Board was anxious to avoid encouraging industries to seek special favours because they were producing important commodities, and at this stage it did not consider the redistribution of manpower to defence

[1] *General Wage Regulation No. 6.* Issued February 27, 1951.
[2] *Ibid.*

plants a matter requiring its urgent attention. This aspect of the Board's policy followed the principle set by the War Labour Board; it was in sharp contrast to the British White Paper of 1948, which emphasized the undermanning of an essential industry as a major reason justifying a wage increase.

Though the public and industry members of the Board thought that the ten per cent allowance was a fair attempt to correct the inequities that had arisen because of the disparities in the movement of wages and salaries, and the rise in the cost of living in the pre-freeze period, they also recognized that it was likely that the cost of living would go on rising and promised to review this policy in the light of the April 1951 index number of the official consumer price index, before July 1st. The trade unions were not prepared to accept a 'catch up' ten per cent, insisting that it should be at least twelve, and they withdrew their representatives in protest. But it was not so much this particular policy of the Wage Stabilization Board that influenced their decision as distrust of Mr Wilson, the Director of Defence Mobilization, who was not regarded as a friend of organized labour; they were also dissatisfied at their relative exclusion from the administrative and policy-making machinery which Wilson had built up to carry out the defence mobilization programme. The trade unions demanded a greater degree of representation throughout this organization and pressed for direct access to the President which they had enjoyed with Mr Roosevelt in wartime—instead of having to go through Mr Wilson's office. A united labour movement determined not to take any further part in the organization of the defence effort unless its grievances were alleviated raised serious political problems for Mr Truman. He met them by appointing a National Advisory Board on Mobilization Policy, on which labour was equally represented with industry, with the function of advising him directly on any aspect of the defence programme.[1]

One of the first decisions of the National Advisory Board was to recommend that the Wage Stabilization Board, which had ceased to function after the trade unions had walked out, should be reconstituted with eighteen members instead of nine, with six drawn from industry, six from the trade unions, and six to represent the public interest. This was accepted and a new Board was set up, the opportunity being taken to appoint a fresh chairman who was not associated with the previous conflict. A further concession won by the

[1] Other concessions were also made. Representatives of the trade unions were appointed as personal advisers to the directors of all the main agencies which had been established.

unions was that in future the Board would have authority, under certain conditions, to settle disputes which threatened to interrupt defence production. The precedent of the War Labour Board was not, however, followed to the extent that the Wage Stabilization Board was given power to intervene in a dispute on its own initiative.

Disputes could be submitted to the Board, either by agreement on both sides, when, if so desired, the Board could give a binding award, or by the President after he had certified that the dispute constituted a threat to defence production—in which case the Board had power only to recommend terms of settlement.[1] This additional function of the Board did not replace other procedures for settling disputes but was supplementary to them; it did, however, cause a certain amount of departmental jealousy and gave rise to criticism from members of the Republican Party who saw in the new provision an attempt to circumvent certain aspects of the bitterly contested Taft-Hartley Act, which, indeed, was the reason why the trade unions were anxious for the change. This aspect of the Board's work did not prove to be as important as the unions had expected.

Cost of Living
Outstanding among the problems which the Board had to tackle was that of the cost of living sliding-scale agreements which affected the wages of over three million workers. This question was extremely explosive, for it was a basic element in the five-year contract between the United Automobile Workers' Union and the General Motors Corporation, which had been signed in 1949, and Mr Reuther, the President of the UAW, made it clear that his union would not be prepared to continue with the rest of its agreement—which promised three more strike-free years—if the Board abrogated this clause. During the interim between the old and the new Boards Mr Johnston bowed to this pressure and issued an order permitting cost of living agreements to exceed the ten per cent formula if they had been negotiated before the wage freeze.[2] This decision was obviously discriminatory against those workers who were not on cost of living sliding scales and encouraged the unions to press for further concessions. The same kind of difficulties were experienced in

[1] Under the Conditions of Employment and National Arbitration Order, SR & O 1305, which was in existence throughout the wage-restraint period in Britain, the Minister of Labour was empowered to refer a dispute to the National Arbitration Tribunal (after certain conditions had been fulfilled); only if he failed to refer a reported dispute within twenty-one days were strikes legal.
[2] *General Wage Regulation No. 8*, March 8, 1951.

Britain during the wage-restraint period when unions refused to abandon their rights to increases under cost of living agreements.[1]

The Evolution of Policy

On April 24, 1951, Wage Adjustment Order No. 1 was issued by the Board. This order authorized an increase to non-operating railway workers, to which they were entitled under a cost of living sliding-scale agreement made after January 25, 1951, although it exceeded the ten per cent formula of Regulation 6. Then on May 18th the Board made a further concession when it approved an agreement which had been arrived at between the 'Big Four' meat-packing companies and four trade unions, which also exceeded the ten per cent formula. The Board justified the increases on the grounds that these were exceptional cases in which hardship would be inflicted if the formula was strictly followed without making allowance for the fact that the wages of these two groups were lagging behind on the base period of January 1950. It also indicated that it was unfair to treat cost of living agreements more favourably than renegotiated contracts where unions were not on sliding scales. Having made these concessions it was no surprise when the Board reviewed the situation its decisions had created and promulgated a new regulation which permitted wage increases, without authorization being necessary, to an amount not exceeding the rise of the consumer price index from January 1951, in addition to the ten per cent previously allowed.[2]

In the absence of a cost of living agreement with a union an employer was not entitled to give an increase in wages up to the level of the rise in the cost of living provided this was done not more frequently than once every six months. This enabled unions to have a choice of whether they negotiated cost of living agreements or adhered to the reopening of contract negotiations at the end of a period of time—most American collective agreements are on an annual basis—knowing that they would have at least the percentage rise in the cost of living for which to bargain. The advantage of the latter procedure to the unions preferring it was that they did not suffer the automatic reduction in wages required by a sliding-scale agreement should the cost of living fall.

[1] There was some important difference in attitude between the British and American trade unions on this question. The unions in America, whether or not under cost-of-living agreements, were united in pressing the Wage Stabilization Board to take the rise in the cost-of-living into account when formulating its policies. In Britain those unions not on sliding scale agreements were critical of those that were, for jeopardizing the wage-restraint policy by their refusal to forgo wage increases.

[2] *General Regulation No.* 8 (Revised) Cost of Living Increases, August 23, 1951.

With the adoption of this regulation the Wage Stabilization Board made the cost of living the basic factor determining future wage changes. In the light of its decisions it was almost certain that the Board would have revised its ten per cent. formula to give all unions the benefits enjoyed by those with cost of living agreements, but the amendment by Congress, in July 1951, of the Defence Production Act, which forced the Office of Price Stabilization to raise its price ceilings on many commodities, made this step inevitable. When signing the amendments to the Act the President, who had opposed them, stated that 'to the extent that this Act permits prices and the cost of living to rise, it will be necessary to allow reasonable adjustment in wages'.

The Board had linked wage movements to the cost of living, but this aspect of the wage problem was not the only factor to which it had to pay regard. On his retirement as Chairman of the Wage Stabilization Board, Dr George W. Taylor, stated that 'in developing its policies, the WSB has not only the objective of wage stabilization, but must also keep in mind three others—the preservation of industrial relations stability, the preservation of collective bargaining to the fullest possible extent, and the fostering of maximum defence production. Policies developed by the Board must represent a balancing of these four objectives. They cannot be focused on a single objective.'[1]

Balancing these objectives implied that the Wage Stabilization Board would not attempt to impose a predetermined wages pattern, but, as far as possible, would allow wage levels to be decided by collective bargaining. Although the Board had laid down general principles to be followed, it in practice permitted pressure from unions and employers to determine relative wage movements. By far the largest number of cases to come before the Wage Stabilization Board were demands to allow firms to adjust their wage rates so as to bring them into line with other firms competing for scarce labour. During an inflationary period, when the labour force is fully occupied and profits are high, wage rates tend to move closer together. If workers do not obtain the same rates as prevail elsewhere they will adopt an aggressive policy to get them, or seek better paid employment, so that employers are also anxious to bring their wage levels up. In effect, the policies of the Wage Stabilization Board during the summer of 1951 worked to prevent the narrowing of wage differentials between plants that would have taken place had wage movements been free of the limits imposed by the ten per cent formula. Although the Board had made provision to meet cases of 'base date abnormalities' and the

[1] *A Report on Wage Stabilization.* WSB, August 1951.

'rare and unusual' cases where shortage of manpower was hampering defence production, these exceptions did not constitute a solution to the general problem of so-called 'inter-plant inequities'. Many firms with plants engaged on defence contracts were also producing goods for civilian use, and wage rates for similar grades of skill employed under the same roof could not be separated according to the destination of the job without causing industrial unrest. If wage rates had been allowed to rise in a plant simply because it had obtained a defence contract this would have been discriminatory against others less fortunately situated, even though they might be producing similar civilian goods.

After considering the problem for some time the Board devised a formula to meet the demands which was based on finding 'an appropriate group of establishments in an appropriate industry or area with whose rates the petitioner's rates are to be compared. This comparison group of establishments shall be the one which is best adapted to preserve normal patterns of wage settings'.[1] This phase of the Board's policy followed previous major decisions which had been based on accepting key agreements as anchor points for its policy. It served to solve the problem of inter-plant inequities, but only at the expense of being more inflationary than stabilizing, since the unions regarded as 'normal patterns' those wage levels set by the organizations which usually led the others in settling new rates. This policy of correcting inequities by allowing those behind always to catch up the leaders was a serious threat to the Board's stabilization objective; everything depended on the ability of the Board to control key wage contracts and this, for political reasons, proved very difficult.

Another problem which confronted the Wage Stabilization Board was that posed by union demands for pension, health, and welfare programmes. Since the United Mineworkers' Union and the Union of Automobile Workers had set the pattern with agreements which secured these benefits, company-provided schemes of the pension and welfare type had become major objectives of collective bargaining. During the summer of 1951 the Board set up a special sub-committee to study this problem. The public members, supported by the trade-union representatives, recommended that health and insurance plans should be virtually free of control, and that company-provided pension schemes should only require the approval of the Board if they were clearly to go beyond a pattern already established in the industry where they were to be introduced. The industry members of the sub-committee issued a minority report which stated that 'The setting up of new programmes and the liberalizing of existing programmes

[1] Wage Stabilization Board release 117, September 28, 1951.

under today's circumstances will have inflationary effects'.[1] They therefore recommended that all new benefit schemes, unless the employee was to pay at least half of the net cost, or where they were merely an extension of an existing programme to a further group of workers, by the same employer, should be subject to the approval of the Board.

Pressure on the Board came not only from the trade unions; employers were equally as concerned that the policy of the Board should not result in a freezing of wage and salary relationships, inside the factory, which would make it difficult for managements to encourage incentive and responsibility. The Board, after consideration of these questions, issued a regulation which laid down rules under which an employer could make adjustments of wages for merit, performance, length of service, promotion, new and changed jobs, overtime, and other special cases.[2] Employers were permitted to continue past practices, but not to exceed the total amount of their wages bill used to meet these special payments in 1950; or they could if they wished adopt a 'six per cent plan' which limited the total of such additions to six per cent of the aggregate straight time rates of the employees in a working group. The aim of this regulation was to provide the maximum degree of flexibility, yet prevent employers from making a 'flank assault upon stabilization'.[3]

Although the wages of union members were protected against a runaway cost of living, by the decision of the Wage Stabilization Board to allow wages to be adjusted by an amount equivalent to any price rise that might occur, the unions were not satisfied. They argued that this ruling meant that wages not only always lagged behind any increase in the consumer price index, but that to limit wages in this way denied workers the right to benefit from improvements in efficiency. Had wages simply followed living costs since 1939, the average earnings of AF of L trade unionists, which were $60.80 for a forty-hour week in April 1951, would have been only $46.10, said a senior AF of L official.[4] Soon afterwards the AF of L members of the Board proposed that the Board should 'approve the policy of permitting wage and salary increases which result from more efficient production'.

The Board approved of incentive payments but sought to prevent the creation of another loophole by insisting that such payments should not normally result in any increase of unit labour cost unless

<hr/>

[1] *New York Times*, November 1, 1951.
[2] *General Wage Regulation No. 5 (revised)*, August 6 and August 17, 1951.
[3] *A Report on Wage Stabilization*, W S B, August 31, 1951.
[4] *Monthly Labour Review*, October 1951.

it could be shown that the expected level of earnings would not be unstabilizing and would not create intra-plant inequities.

A far more difficult question was posed by the agreement between the United Automobile Workers' Union and the General Motors Corporation. This agreement, which ran for five years, provided that employees should receive a four cents per hour yearly increase, based on a calculation of expected annual gains in productivity. Four cents per hour was well above the one cent per hour allowed for every one per cent increase in the cost of living index, which the Board permitted under its basic formula. The Board eventually decided to allow this agreement, which had been negotiated before January 1951, to be implemented. It also decided to allow other agreements of a similar kind, where it could be shown that the workers covered were linked to groups that had enjoyed annual improvement factor increases prior to 1951. These decisions were announced as 'interim' in character, but in spite of a statement by Mr Eric Johnston to the CIO Convention, that 'production wage increases were fair and reasonable . . . and not unstabilizing',[1] the Board never issued a general wage regulation authorizing this type of agreement in principle. The reluctance of the public members of the Board to define their attitude towards the issue of annual improvement escalators was castigated by labour leaders who accused them of deliberate procrastination.

The pressure on the public members of the Wage Stabilization Board mounted in the second year of its activities. The Board bowed to the power of the unions to the extent of giving the steelworkers permission to enjoy an increase in wages that was said to be larger than the Steelworkers' Union had ever negotiated before. In justification the Board held that the size of the increase only permitted the steelworkers to catch up to workers in other industries who had been granted wage increases in the previous year when the steelworkers had not had any advance.

There was much bitter criticism from certain employers at the concessions which they felt the Board was making to the demands of the unions, although no request for a wage change could go to the Board without the support of the employers concerned. The rock on which the Wage Stabilization Board finally foundered was, appropriately, the man to whom the Board had made its first concession, John L. Lewis. The leader of the United Mineworkers' Union had negotiated a wage increase of $1.90, but the Board ruled that it could only sanction an increase of $1.50. Lewis refused to yield to the authority of the Board and called a strike, whereupon President Truman, on the eve of an election, intervened and overruled the Board in Lewis's

[1] *New York Times*, November 12, 1951.

favour. The Chairman thereupon resigned, and he was followed by the representatives of industry. The Board was dead, though a temporary arrangement was made to keep it going without the representatives from the unions and employees until the incoming Eisenhower finally brought the work of the Board to a close.

Enforcement
The problem of preventing employers from giving concealed wage advances by promotions and special additions had been a considerable headache to the War Labour Board[1] as they are extremely difficult to control; it proved to be no less of a problem for the Wage Stabilization Board. Although penalties for violation of a wage stabilization order were severe, with so many thousands of firms involved and the ramifications of the Board's policy so extensive, it was an almost impossible task to check the accuracy of all details of wage payments filed by employers. If was, therefore, necessary to place a good deal of reliance on their honesty. Some illegal increase of wages was bound to occur, but the Board refused to admit that it was great enough to cause undue alarm.

The Board established a Review and Appeals Committee and appointed Enforcement Commissions, nationally and regionally. The Enforcement Commissions sat in a quasi-judicial capacity to hear cases of alleged violation of the Board's regulations, with the power to subpoena witnesses and take evidence on oath. The duty of bringing charges before the Enforcement Commissions was the function of the Enforcement and Legal Division of the Wage Stabilization Board, which by mid-1951 had over 2,000 cases under review for investigation.[2] The accused had the right to appeal from a regional to the National Enforcement Commission, which was the final judge. The Commissions were free to order an offending employer to 'cease and desist' and to recommend such punishment as they thought fit, which mainly consisted of recommending other Government departments to take action. This could include the cancelling of defence contracts, disallowing excess wages as a charge against income tax, and judicial proceedings. Penalties provided under the Defence Production Act, which could only be imposed by a court, for contraventions of wage-regulation orders were heavy, up to a $10,000 fine, one year in jail, or both.[3] Very little use was made of these powers.

[1] See S. A. Levitan, *Ingrade Wage-Rate Progression in War and Peace*, New York (1950)
[2] Dr G. W. Taylor, *ibid.*
[3] *Enforcement Procedure, Resolution 35*, July 25, 1951.

Administrative Structure

A major complaint against the Wage Stabilization Board in the first year was that it took several months for a petition to be processed. From May to August roughly 3,500 petitions were decided by the Board, but over 7,000 were outstanding at the end of that period. To remedy this situation and decentralize the administration of policy, fourteen regional boards, which were minor editions of the national Board in their composition and function, were set up. A substantial degree of authority was delegated to them, but petitions which raised issues of policy not previously decided by the national Board and certain other issues, such as all petitions coming within the designation of 'rare and unusual' cases, were reserved by the national Board.[1]

The Wage Stabilization Board and each of its regional organizations was serviced by a staff of economic analysts, manpower and other specialists. Each petition for a wage increase was analysed in the light of past decisions and the current economic and industrial situation. The cases were then submitted to the Board, accompanied by the recommendations of the Case Analysis Division, for its ruling. Thus the procedure was one of expert consideration quite unlike the procedure of the British National Arbitration Tribunal and its successor the Industrial Disputes Tribunal. The difference in procedure arose from a difference in function.[2] The Wage Stabilization Board was not primarily a court of equity deciding on questions at issue between two parties. Apart from the occasions when it was specifically asked to act as an arbitration tribunal, the Board was concerned only with the approval, or otherwise, of wage changes already agreed upon by unions and employers, and, indeed, unless petitions were submitted jointly the Board could give no decision, except in cases where no union existed, when an application from an employer alone would be accepted for consideration.

In a survey of the administrative problems which faced the Wage Stabilization Board, M. A. Horowitz, the Director of the Office of Case Analysis, has pointed to the difficulties which arose out of the fact that the Board had a tripartite membership and was based on the principle of voluntary acceptance.[3]

The Director cited a number of weaknesses to which the Board was

---

[1] *Delegation of Authority to Regional Boards, Resolution 64*, September 18, 1951.

[2] Even after the White Paper of 1948 the National Arbitration Tribunal did not change its policy of deciding each case on its merits and it resisted the feeble attempts to push it in the direction of becoming the administrative instrument of a national wages policy.

[3] M. A. Horowitz, 'Administrative Problems of the Wage Stabilization Board', *Industrial and Labour Relations Review*, April 1954.

prone. These included: (1) the undue pressure which could be brought against the independent public members; (2) the delay in policy formulation caused by the attempts to secure agreement between opposed interests; (3) the bad attendance of the industry and trade union members, which caused further delays in decision making; (4) the hostility to the experts on the staff of the Board and the tendency of representatives of both sides of industry to ignore their recommendations; (5) the failure effectively to decentralize.[1]

To these criticisms one of the trade union members of the Board replied, that it was inevitable that a tripartite board should cause some delay. This price had necessarily to be paid for the support by industry of wage controls. The danger that the Board would lose its functions to the experts employed to analyse and process cases was a real one. There was a constant tendency for the staff to encroach on the prerogatives of the Board, which could only be checked by the vigilance and zealous exercise of their responsibilities by the members who were drawn from industry.[2]

A similar problem occurred with the War Labour Board and it is likely to occur with any organization of the same kind. It is the familiar problem of the expert civil servant and political chief. In this case, however, the staff experts were mainly in close sympathy with the public members, to whom they were drawn by bonds of common technical ability and background. The public members of the Board were mainly recruited from the legal profession and the universities, and the expert staff was obtained largely from the same sources. It was thus inevitable that there should be a clash, since the representatives from both sides of industry tended to regard the public members and the expert staff as 'academic' and lacking in an understanding of industrial realities. On the other hand the experts, no doubt, felt that it was their duty to save the public from the folly and sectional greed of both sides of industry.

Evaluation

The Wage Stabilization Board was trying to evolve and administer a national wages policy to combat inflation and assist defence production whilst at the same time attempting to avoid doing violence to collective bargaining and industrial relations. It had, therefore, necessarily to be sensitive to economic and political pressures. In the circumstances of a limited war situation which did not involve the intensity of effort and psychological climate of the second World War, it was difficult to evoke the same level of response to the impo-

[1] *Op. cit.*
[2] Elmer Walker, *Industrial and Labour Relations Review*, April 1955.

sition of wage controls. The unions were not bound by any no-strike pledge, such as they had readily given during World War II; they were not convinced that it was either unpatriotic or against their self-interest to press for higher wages.

The Wage Stabilization Board would have broken down long before its eventual end had it attempted to pursue a stringent policy of restraint. The primary objective of the Board as stated by the last Chairman was the modest one of preventing 'abnormal increases' in wages.[1] In twenty-three months of its existence the Board received over 127,000 cases, of which 115,000 had been disposed of by the end of December 1952. Of these 115,000 cases, 87,000 (75 per cent) were approved, 11,000 (10 per cent) were modified, 11,000 (10 per cent) were disposed of without the Board making a decision, and 6,000 (4 per cent) were rejected. Since these petitions were based on voluntary agreements, or determined unilaterally by employers, 'to compensate for changes in living costs and to meet the competitive pressure of a generally tight labour market'[2] it is clear that the Board was accepting, to a very large extent, the guidance of the market in the making of its decisions. Some unions probably secured less than would otherwise have been the case had the Board not been in the way, and to this extent the front runners were constantly being pushed back. But the average of the field was probably not reduced, since the awards of the Board tended to encourage other unions to demand and obtain the maximum percentage increases—when they might have been content with less—simply because this was the amount to which official fiat decreed they were entitled.

It was the opinion of the Public Members of the Board that in the absence of really effective measures taken by Congress to control inflation at the source, and so to prevent prices from rising, it was impossible to do more than try to prevent the movement of wages from adding much to the inflationary pressure. The Board was helped by the slowing down of the increase in the consumer price index after the stabilization programme had been launched. It was tempting to attribute the slackening of consumer demand to the efforts of the Economic Stabilization Agency, but it was most probably due to the intensive stocking up which took place in the nine months prior to the introduction of the stabilization programme, and a marked increase in private saving.

The record of the Office of Price Stabilization was not wholly dissimilar to that of the Wage Stabilization Board. Faced with a constant economic and political pressure to concede price increases,

[1] *Wage Stabilization Board—Release*, December 16, 1952.
[2] *Ibid.*

TABLE 7

1947–49=100

Manufacturing Industries

	Average Weekly Earnings Index	Consumer Price Index
1947	94.4	95.5
1948	102.2	102.8
1949	103.7	101.8
1950	112.0	102.8
1951	122.0	111.0
1952	128.4	113.5
1953	135.4	114.4
1954	135.7	114.8
1955	144.5	114.5
1956	151.4	116.2

Source: Monthly Labour Review

it made one concession after another. An attempt to prevent wage increases from being used as a reason for raising the price control ceilings was not very successful, and the efforts of the Economic Stabilization Agency, in this respect, were undermined by amendments to the Defence Production Act, which permitted manufacturers to pass on all increases in costs incurred before the end of July 1951.

It will be noted that price stabilizing was not really achieved until after the Wage Stabilization Board had been terminated. Whatever success might be attributed to the Board, stability was really brought about by the cut back in demand after its demise, which resulted in unemployment rising from 1.3 million, in October 1952, to 2.7 million in October 1954.

The attempt to stabilize wages was far more thorough-going in the United States than the comparable effort made by the Labour Government in Britain. Whether its record is regarded as a success or a failure, the policy of wage controls exercised by an independent Board demonstrated the limitations of this type of attack on the problem of inflation in a free society.[1] The history of the Wage Stabilization Board is a record of a series of jumps from expedient to expedient, and it is not possible, merely by dignifying each temporary base with a title, and suggesting that the jump had been made in accordance with a fundamental principle, to hide the fact that the main occupation of the Board was a vain attempt to stop leaks in the policy of stabilization. The fact was that neither employers nor unions were prepared to accept cuts in incomes imposed by an administrative machine in the absence of a compelling crisis situation.

[1] For a discussion of this issue see 'Governmental Wage Restraints: Their Limits and Uses in a Mobilized Economy', a paper by Clark Kerr, and comments by R. A. Lester and Dale Yoder, Papers and Proceedings of the American Economic Association, 1951.

F

In these circumstances the task of the independent public members becomes little more than that of mediators who seek to establish settlements which will satisfy both sides without causing a stoppage of work. The wage levels which result cannot be very far away from the levels that the pressures in the market would in any event determine. If they were they would be unacceptable to one or the other of the parties. Thus it is extremely difficult for a national wages board to achieve the object of stability without violating other objectives, such as the alleviation of manpower shortages and industrial peace. In the event it is the object of stability which usually has to give way, since stability demands the maintenance of the *status quo* in the face of a dynamic situation which cannot be controlled without paying the price of saying no. In the United States—a democracy—this price proved to be that of allowing wages to rise to the levels indicated by the market; in a dictatorship it would be possible to buttress a policy of wage restraint by totalitarian controls, but even under such conditions inflation cannot be totally suppressed by the exercise of administrative authority.

As a temporary expedient, wage restraint may be of great significance simply because it slows down the immediate wage responses, but crisis psychology tends to dissipate rapidly and it is essential that self-interest and public interest should be equated if the long-term policy is to be successful. Great as the differences in American and British methods were, they had one thing in common; that ultimately they both rested on the willingness of employers and unions to accept and abide by the policy decisions of the authorities. American policy, which was at bottom a voluntary policy of wage restraint, in spite of its legalistic framework, suffered the same fate as its British counterpart. It was abandoned by both sides when it failed to suit their economic interests. The lesson was not that the attempts to run a national wage policy were futile, but that controls alone will not prevent inflation in conditions of full employment and excess demand.

CHAPTER 6

Wage Policy in Sweden

The system of industrial relations is more centralized in Sweden than in either Britain or America, but less centralized than it is in Holland. Collective bargaining takes place generally on an industry-wide basis, but clerical and supervisory workers have their own organizations and are covered by separate agreements.[1] A distinguishing feature of wage settlement in Sweden is the role played by the central trade union and employers' organizations.

The Swedish Trades Union Federation, LO (Landsorganisationen), consists of forty-four affiliated unions, with a membership of 1.4 million, most of whom are manual workers. The central organization of the non-manual clerical and salaried employees, TCO (Tjänstemännens Centralorganisation) has forty-two unions affiliated, with a membership of 350,000. Swedish employers are almost as well organized as their employees and SAF (Svenska Arbetsgirareförenin-gen), has affiliated to it forty-three associations with 15,000 members, which employ three-quarters of a million workers in mainly manufac-turing and building industries. In addition there are several other employers' organizations, which work in close conjunction with SAF.

Each of the three central organizations exercises an influence over their constituents which far exceeds the power of the British TUC and of the British Employers' Confederation. The authority of the central organizations has arisen out of the historical circumstances of Sweden's industrial and social development.[2] An important feature of the Swedish situation is that the LO has a central strike fund, con-tributed by the unions, and used to support any union with a strike on its hands.[3] To safeguard the central organization, permission must be obtained from the LO Executive Council, before a strike is called, if more than three per cent of the members are affected. If this proce-dure is not followed, then the union as a consequence forfeits the

[1] For a detailed account, see Paul H. Norgren *The Swedish Collective Bargain-ing System*, Harvard (1941).
[2] Cf. Norgren, *op. cit.*
[3] The LO normally contributes about 25 per cent of the benefit paid by a union to its members on strike.

support of the LO and is deprived of strike assistance from the central fund.

SAF, the central employers' organization, has a similar central lockout and indemnity fund, which enables it to insist on each affiliated organization obtaining approval from the central body before an agreement is signed. This device is an influential instrument for preventing an affiliated organization from pursuing a different policy from that of the SAF

Affiliation to the central organizations of the unions and employers is, in both cases, on a voluntary basis, but the influence and authority which the LO and SAF enjoy has enabled them to negotiate together on behalf of all their members. Wage policy has become one of the most important functions of the central organizations and the agreements into which they enter now provide a framework within which changes are determined at the industrial level. This approach to the problem of wage policy contrasts with the limited discretion of the British TUC. On no occasion have British unions shown any sign that they would, under any circumstances, be willing to allow the TUC to enter into an agreement which would bind them to accept its terms. There have, however, been suggestions that the TUC ought to be empowered to formulate and enforce, in the interests of the whole trade union movement, a national wages policy, and envious eyes have been cast at the position enjoyed by the LO. Remote as the chance seems to be of the TUC acquiring the necessary power to emulate the LO, the likelihood of the British Employers' Confederation achieving a position of authority similar to that which the SAF has secured is even more inconceivable. Nevertheless it is worth examining the Swedish experience in the field of national wage policy, since from it much might be learned that would be applicable even in the different circumstances which prevail in Britain.

Wages Policy in the 1930's
The Swedish Employers' Federation, SAF, took the initiative, in 1931, after the onset of the depression, of proposing a wage policy designed to reduce the costs of labour in five major export industries. The LO was not exactly enthusiastic about the idea, but it was persuaded by the employers' pledge that the reductions would be restricted to the bare minimum. On this basis the LO persuaded the constituent unions to accept cuts which over all the industries averaged five per cent. This did not, in fact, amount to a cut in real wages for those in employment, since prices had fallen to a far greater extent. Wages remained unchanged throughout 1933 and 1934, although in the latter year prices had started to rise substantially. In 1935,

as business went on improving, the unions pressed for the restoration of the cut made in 1931, and money wages advanced by five per cent; in 1937 wages were increased by, on the average, a further eight per cent. It is widely believed by the unions and the employers that this anti-depression wage policy was highly successful, and both central organizations of unions and employers were in agreement that they should develop the practice of making long-term wage policy plans as an antidote to the trade cycle.

The trade union interest in planning wages from an over-all national point of view, rather than allowing them to be settled by sectional bargaining, was further emphasized by the adoption, in 1937, of a 'solidarity wage policy'. The object of this policy was to narrow the difference between the wages in the lowest-paid and the highest-paid industries. The leaders of the LO proposed that the unions concerned with the sawmill and wood pulp industries should seek a lower wage increase so that the workers employed in the lumber industry, who were notoriously underpaid, could obtain a correspondingly larger increase. By this means, it was agreed, the total cost of labour in the final product would be changed little or not at all. In the event, the unions were persuaded to accept this plan, and the employers eventually agreed to increase the wages of lumber workers by twenty per cent and the wages of sawmill and pulp workers by only eight per cent.

The stress on equality has been one of the chief characteristics of the wage policy of the Swedish unions ever since the 1930's.[1] It is a natural concomitant of the marked egalitarian trends which have been a feature of Sweden's social and economic policy for the past half-century. The unions have sought to justify their strongly held ethical notion that wage and salary differences should be reduced to the minimum by the psychological argument that narrow differentials would make for greater stability. In their opinion wide differences create a sense of injustice and strong pressures to revise wage structures. Swedish employers have been far from enthusiastic supporters of the trade union point of view, and the course of events would seem to indicate that they have reasonable grounds for their scepticism of the soundness of a wage structure as egalitarian as that desired by the unions.

Wage Differentials
The narrowing of differentials between the wages of skilled and unskilled workers, between manual and clerical workers, and between

[1] The origins of the solidarity policy in fact go back to a resolution passed at the LO congress in 1922.

men and women workers, as well as the levelling up of wages of one industry compared with another, is not a course of development that is confined to countries that have pursued national wage policies. It is a feature of industrial and social progress almost everywhere. Generally the widest differentials are to be found in underdeveloped countries; this is simply because skill and education can command a high scarcity price. The normal trend of events is for differentials to narrow as education is diffused through the community, the labour market becomes more open and competitive, and as technological change continuously breaks down attempts to maintain monopolistic control of occupations.[1] The development of trade unions and industry-wide wage structures has reinforced the trends generated by more fundamental economic and social forces in most countries except Russia. Narrowing has occurred even in the Soviet Union, but there has been a powerful effort to maintain the widest possible differentials, in order to encourage production by highly rewarding effort, skill and responsibility.

Table 8 indicates that differentials have continued to narrow since 1939. It is, however, generally thought that the levelling process has tapered off; in this respect Sweden is not different from Britain and other countries. There would seem to be limits, which are set by economic and social circumstances, to the extent to which it is possible to force wage structures into a particular mould. Whether it be attempts to maintain wide differentials, as in the Soviet Union, or narrow differentials, as in Sweden, market pressures cannot be entirely circumvented by planned wages policies.[2] It is admitted by trade union supporters that the slowing down of the narrowing trend, and in certain cases its reversal, is due to economic factors and, in some degree, to a change in trade union and employer policy,

TABLE 8[3]

	Hourly earnings				Clerical		
	Manufacturing industries		Agriculture	Lumber	Manufacturing		
	Men	Women	Men	Men	Men	Women	Foremen
1939	100	100	100	100	100	100	100
1945	142	150	184	181	141	146	135
1950	204	229	290	257	200	216	188
1955	346	382	485	491	323	356	295

[1] Cf. A. G. B. Fisher, 'Education and Relative Wage Rates', *International Review*, June 1932; E. H. Phelps Brown, 'The Why and Wherefore of Wage Differentials', *Personnel Management*, June 1956.

[2] See L. G. Reynolds and C. H. Taft, *The Evolution of Wage Structure* (1956).

[3] Based on data given by G. Rehn, 'Swedish Wages and Wage Policies', *The Annals of the American Academy of Political and Social Science*, March 1957. This chapter owes a great deal to the work of Mr Rehn.

brought about by a growing resistance on the part of the higher paid wage and salaries workers to further levelling.

Wartime Wage Policy

Although Sweden maintained her traditional policy of neutrality during the war, her economy was almost as seriously affected as were the economies of some of the belligerents. In December, 1939, under the influence of the war situation, the leaders of the SAF and the LO met together and agreed upon a national wage policy for the duration of the crisis. The essence of this agreement was that at the end of each quarter all wage rates laid down in collective agreements would be adjusted according to changes in the cost of living index. As a result of the initiative taken by the central organizations the cost of living sliding scale was incorporated into most of the existing agreements. Up to the autumn of 1942 the cost of living had risen by thirty-three per cent above the 1939 level, and, under the sliding-scale arrangement, wages had risen by about twenty-five per cent. In view of the steadily worsening economic situation it was decided to stabilize prices and wages at their prevailing levels. Agricultural and forestry workers were excluded from the wage freeze, and in 1942 and 1943 other low wage groups were allowed special increases. In addition there was a small but steady general increase in wages during the war amounting to about $1\frac{1}{2}$ per cent per year, which was due to overtime, up-grading, piece rate earnings, merit rates and other allowances. By 1945, prices had risen by forty-one per cent, and the wages of male workers in manufacturing industries by forty-two per cent, in agriculture by eighty-four per cent, and forestry by eighty-one per cent, though the previously high wages in building and construction had only gone up by twenty-seven per cent. The net effect of the wartime stabilization policy had been to narrow the differential between the high and low paid workers.

The Post-war Boom

The LO, at the end of the war, recommended the unions to press for a reduction of prices rather than to unstabilize the general level of wages. But the membership of most unions had become restless under the restraints imposed by the stabilization programme and there was an immediate demand for higher wages. Efforts were made to secure larger increases for the lower-paid workers, in conformity with the LO policy; over all the increases secured amounted to about five per cent. Again, in 1946, the LO sought to persuade the unions not to jeopardize the system of price controls by excessive wage demands. Earnings in manufacturing industry, however, climbed during the year by about nine per cent, but prices only went up on the official index by two per cent. The inflationary pressure which had been steadily building up was now felt with full force; wages rose by no less than fourteen per cent in 1947, and it became impossible to hold prices down to an insignificant rise.

Alarmed by the situation which had developed, the Government held discussions with both sides of industry and an appeal was made for wage restraint. In support of the appeal, regulations limiting the payments of dividends by public companies were introduced and company profits tax was increased from thirty-eight to forty-seven per cent. The LO was not able, however, to curb the pressure of demand for higher incomes and when the annual negotiations came round the unions obtained substantial increases in wages and salaries. Faced by the prospect of a further fall in the foreign currency reserves, due to excessive consumer demand generated by the rise in wage and salary incomes, the Government decided to reduce the public's purchasing power by excise taxes, and also by a cut in investments, brought about by administrative controls, and in the 1947–48 financial year a budget surplus which covered capital as well as operating expenditure was achieved.

Wage Stabilization

The measures taken by the Government slowed down the rate at which prices had been increasing and they also convinced the LO that it was futile for unions to secure large increases in money wages only to have them nullified by higher taxes and price increases. The Executive Council of the LO therefore called upon all the affiliated unions to stabilize the situation by consenting to extend existing agreements for a further twelve months. The central organization of the white-collar workers' unions, TCO, also made a similar recommendation to its affiliates, and a strong lead was given by the Civil Servants who decided not to take advantage of an increase in salary of three per cent to which they were entitled as a result of the increase in the cost of living.

The amount of wage increases negotiated in 1949 was fractional and it was decided to continue the stabilization policy in 1950. The agreement not to make wage demands did not mean that wages were prevented entirely from rising. Since employment was full and labour was in short supply employers were willing to pay more to obtain what they required, so the wage drift continued. Rising production also meant larger pay packets, as two-thirds of the Swedish industrial labour force were paid according to results.

The object of the wage 'freeze' had been to bring about an im-

TABLE 9

Adult Males

	Contractual Wage Increase	Wage Drift	Total earnings	Consumer Prices	Unemployment[1] excluding Building Trades	Produc- tion
	Per cent	Per cent	Per cent	Per cent	Per cent	Per cent
1946	3.2	4.8	8.0	1.9	3.3	20.5
1947	9.7	4.4	14.1	3.3	2.9	3.7
1948	4.5	3.8	8.3	4.4	2.9	5.7
1949	0.2	2.8	3.0	1.8	2.9	3.8
1950	—	3.9	3.9	1.1	2.3	3.8
1951	14.3	6.3	20.6	15.4	1.9	5.0
1952	11.6	6.6	18.2	8.2	2.6	—2.4
1953	1.1	2.5	3.6	1.4	2.8	1.2
1954	1.5	2.9	4.4	.7	2.6	4.2
1955	4.3	4.2	8.5	3.1	2.5	6.3
1956	4.3	3.5	8.0	4.5	2.9	2.8

Sources: *Index, Svenska Handelsbanken. Konjunkturjournalen. Statistisk Arsbok*

provement in Sweden's balance of payments situation, and this was achieved, but the devaluation of the Swedish currency in 1949 put a pressure on the price level that could not be for long offset by subsidies. The outbreak of the Korean War, with its influence on world prices, added to the difficulty of keeping the cost of living steady. But the factors which finally shattered the stabilization programme were the distortions of the wage structure and the dissatisfactions that were created by the arbitrary effects of the wage freeze. The LO had to agree that wage stability was no longer a tenable policy and, with the Government, it watched the inevitable 'wage explosion' with trepidation. However, the Government and the LO realized that it was impossible to prevent the upsurge in wage increases by administrative measures without creating a first-class political crisis at a moment of tense international activity. In the circumstances, the Government and the LO decided to put on a bold face, and the situation was hopefully described as a 'once and for all inflation'.

A rise in wages of twenty per cent, and, when taxes were included, of the cost of living by nineteen per cent, was not an experience that made a great deal of sense to anyone. The unions believed that since there had been a rise in productivity prices ought not to have gone up so much and the LO informed the central employers' organization, SAF, that unless provision was made to re-open any agreements arrived at, the demands of the unions would again be substantial. The employers replied that they would be prepared to make some

[1] Unemployment percentages are based in Sweden on trade union membership. The total figures are affected by the high seasonal level of unemployment that occurs in winter in Sweden owing to the northern latitude of the country.

arrangement of the kind proposed only if the unions would agree to concluding one master agreement which would regulate all wage changes. The LO could not, it claimed, persuade its member unions to agree to this course. At this stage the Government sought to persuade the unions to limit their demands to such a scale as would keep total earnings to a level not more than five per cent higher. The LO replied that to carry out this suggestion was impossible, since it was not in keeping with the state of the labour market and the general economic situation.

The two central bodies continued negotiations and a complicated agreement was eventually reached. In spite of the fact that this agreement permitted unions to obtain substantial increases of eight per cent for men and ten per cent for women, with further exceptions in special cases, it aroused considerable antagonism among certain member unions. In one instance the LO had to threaten to withhold any support when a union appeared intent on a strike to enforce its demands for a larger increase. By the end of 1952 wages by negotiation had risen by approximately twelve per cent, but the pressures in the labour market pulled total wage earnings up to a total of eighteen per cent. Thus wages had risen by thirty-eight per cent in two years, but in the same period industrial production had only gone up by a trivial 2.5 per cent.

Wage Restraint and Reaction Again
The two years of massive wage and price increases were now followed by a further period of wage restraint. The change in the attitude of the unions was encouraged by a change in the economic climate; at the beginning of 1953 unemployment was higher than at any time since the end of the war. As will be seen from Table 9 unemployment remained higher than it had been in 1951 for the next few years.

In an endeavour to keep labour costs from rising the Government asked the unions to be as moderate in their demands as possible. The Swedish employers' organization interpreted the Government's desire as limiting wage increases to no more than three per cent. The unions resented this attempt to curb their demands and there were mutterings of strike threats as the atmosphere thickened with the rumours of counter-action by the Government.

The final outcome of the annual negotiations was an agreement which provided for a seven per cent increase in wages. The threat of large-scale stoppages had been sufficient to persuade the employers that wage increases were less costly than lost orders. Wage advances obtained by the unions affiliated to the LO had normally been of much greater significance than those obtained by the white-collar unions; the pay of the latter usually lagged behind and salary revisions were on a firm-to-firm basis. In 1955, however, the TCO unions, under pressure from their members, who were in revolt at continually being behind, negotiated an agreement for a seven per cent salary increase, which laid down a minimum that was widely emulated.[1]

The Government, fearing the effect of this round of wage and salary increases, decided upon the drastic step of reducing purchasing power by two per cent by means of compulsory savings. This idea, similar to the one suggested by Lord Keynes during the second World War, was not, however, put into effect, despite support from the LO, because it aroused political opposition, which threatened to disrupt the Coalition Government. Finding that its actions in this direction were blocked, the Government turned to another. Profits tax was increased, credit restrictions were made more onerous and the rate of interest was raised.

Prices had risen in 1955 by three per cent and it was feared that they would rise much more in 1956 unless the pace at which incomes were rising could be held in check. After joint discussions the LO, TCO and SAF decided that they would agree upon a wage increase for all manual and salaried workers of four per cent; again, however, the pressures of the labour market led to a wage drift of almost the same magnitude as the negotiated increase. The effect of this increase in incomes was to raise prices by another five per cent.

Swedish Attitudes to Wage Policy under Full Employment
The problem of maintaining economic stability under conditions of full employment, and in relation to this aim, the kind of wage policy that should be pursued has, perhaps, been given more attention by the Swedish trade union organization than that of any other country, with the exception of Holland. At the end of the war the LO was of the opinion that full employment accompanied by stability could be maintained by the use of fiscal policy, a co-ordinated wage policy and the use of subsidies and price controls. Special emphasis was placed on the factor of greater equality, both in general distribution of incomes and between one wage and another. Greater equality was desired both for its own sake and because it was believed that inequality only encouraged wage demands to redress the injustice that was felt by the lower-paid workers.[2]

The passion for equality has resulted in an egalitarian income

[1] G. Rehn, 'Swedish Wages and Wage Policies', *op. cit.*
[2] See *Trade Unions and Full Employment* published by the LO and G. Rehn, 'Unionism and Wages Structure in Sweden', *The Theory of Wage Determination* (1957).

distribution and a substantial narrowing of wage differentials,[1] but there is no evidence that this development has contributed towards economic stability. It is well within the bounds of possibility that the concentration on equalization has, contrary to the LO belief, contributed to the excessive pressure of wage demands in Sweden. The demand for wage increases generated by a desire to correct an over-equalized wage structure may be just as powerful as those which are cited by the advocates of levelling as arising from a situation in which differences are too great.

The Swedes have never, in practice, sought to follow the example of Holland and adopt a centrally determined system of job evaluation. In the words of Rehn, 'they have felt it rational to leave room for compromises between equality and the market'.[2] It is admitted that the LO has been compelled to retreat by the behaviour of the labour market and the attitude of union members, from carrying the policy of equalization as far as was thought by the LO to be theoretically desirable.[3]

The level at which wages have been set by collective agreement, even in the years of the most rapid advance, has been below that which the market established. It will be seen from Table 9 that each year there has been a considerable wage drift. In other words, firms with full order books and in a strong competitive position have been prepared to pay more to obtain the labour that they required, and it goes almost without saying that their employees have been only too willing to accept what the market would bear.

The wage drift has been the subject of considerable study in Sweden,[4] and the economists of the LO, SAF and the Government have now reached such a stage of sophisticated analysis that the likely amount of wage drift is taken into account in wage negotiations. The constant tendency for wages to creep ahead of negotiated levels is not regarded by the trade union leaders with equanimity, since they feel that they are being called upon to agree to settlements which are below what employers are prepared to pay. 'If considerable wage-drifting occurs during a period of wage-freeze or restraint in wage claims, this has a threefold effect: members consider that the organization is not properly looking after their interests; distrust arises between the groups enjoying wage-drifting and those whose wage system prevents them from getting it. Finally the authority of the

[1] Reynolds and Taft, op. cit.
[2] Rehn, 'Unionism and Wage Structure in Sweden', op. cit.
[3] Swedish Wages and Wage Policies', op. cit.
[4] See B. Hansen and G. Rehn, 'On Wage Drift: A Problem of Money-Wage Dynamics', Twenty-five Economic Essays in Honour of Erik Lindahl (1956).

WAGE POLICY IN SWEDEN

Confederation of Trade Unions is reduced both *vis-à-vis* the national unions and *vis-à-vis* the community, as it has shown itself incapable of managing its wages policy.'[1] Trade unions must then, in the opinion of the LO, make perfectly clear that their functions and responsibilities do not extend to accepting an unconditional duty of maintaining national economic stability. The principal task of a trade union is to protect the interest of its members, just as it is the principal task of a company to make and sell goods at a profit. It does not follow that a trade union or an employer has no responsibility to the public; it means simply that a trade union can only accept wider responsibilities to the extent that it does not seriously undermine its ability to discharge its fundamental duties to its own members.

The LO rejects as an alternative to the settlement of wages by the trade unions and employers any notion of the State assuming this responsibility. If the State were to determine wages directly, the trade unions would inevitably be weakened, since they would lose one of their most vital functions. Trade unions were incorporated into the machinery of the State by the Soviet Union and Nazi Germany, in order to make certain that they were not able, *inter alia*, to pursue wages policies that would, almost certainly, at some point, conflict with the policy of the State. The wage drift was prevented by curtailing the personal freedom of the individual worker so that it was difficult to obtain a wage increase by threatening to leave and find a job elsewhere.[2]

If, then, the control of wages by the State is to be shunned, does it follow that continuous inflation must be accepted as the price of maintaining collective bargaining under conditions of full employment? The LO firmly rejects the doctrine, advocated by the American economist, Sumner Slichter, and others, that 'a continuous mild inflation' is the simplest way of maintaining full employment. The reason for their opinion is not that they think wage earners will be hit more severely by a fall in the value of money; on the contrary, it is probable that wage earners will be least hit, since the unions are quite capable of obtaining commensurate wage increases. It is 'interest on fixed capital, pensions and other fixed incomes (that will) walk up the stairs, while prices and wages go up in the lift'.[3]

The real danger of inflation to workers is the effect that it may have

---

[1] *Trade Unions and Full Employment*, LO (1953).

[2] With the lifting of the most onerous restrictions in recent years there has developed in the opinion of one highly qualified observer a considerable wage drift that may well soon cause the Soviet authorities difficulties similar to those experienced in the West.

[3] *Trade Unions and Full Employment*.

on the productive capacity of the country, since the resources of a country cannot be utilized in the most adequate way during an inflation. 'Efforts to maintain a stable price level through price control under inflationary pressure are, quite naturally, concentrated upon goods affecting the cost of living index, and this can easily lead to changes in production which are not desirable from the point of view of the national economy. The risk of quality deterioration is also great. Non-essential industries, where price control is less strict or less effective, are likely to draw away labour from other, perhaps far more important, branches of production and trade. Even public investment control is insufficient and notoriously not very effective regarding small firms, which can often be housed in already existing premises or expand in defiance of regulations.

'Another long-term result is that the value of savings is undermined by price increases. At short sight, this may appear advantageous for the wage earners, as it increases their share of the national income at the expense of those who use up their saved capital or the interest on it. But if the policy of full employment is to be based on continuous price increases—or result in them—this will cause persons with savings to place them in goods instead of money assets, a tendency which, by increasing the money value of the former, is liable to cause economic confusion. Persons with small savings are not, as a rule, able to place their money so that it is protected against value deterioration, and are consequently unfairly treated.

'Also in other respects, it is obvious that a constant rise in prices is not, in the long run, reconcilable with economic stability: instead of increasing production by normal rationalization methods, private enterprise concentrates upon speculating in the general price increase, by hoarding up goods needed for current production, in order to sell them at artificially inflated prices. This results in a distribution of incomes favouring persons whose activities are of little value or even directly detrimental to the national economy. Saving—whether it applies to money, materials or manpower—becomes less attractive or even means losses. It is clear that such a development cannot benefit the wage earners, even if, thanks to rapid nominal wage increases, they succeed in retaining their share of the national income. The actual fall in productivity or the reduction in the rate of increase of efficiency is bound ultimately to hit them also.'[1]

In the light of this penetrating analysis of the problems which full employment in a democratic society present to trade unions, the LO come to the following conclusion: 'Since the problem of balancing the national economy cannot, in the long run, be solved by means of

[1] *Trade Unions and Full Employment.*

regulations of the present type (i.e. a number of negative controls, which have a greatly varying effectiveness and therefore a distorting effect on production), one should remove the prospects private enterprise has of making exaggerated profits, by means of a deliberate monetary, fiscal and wage policy.'[1]

Price controls are rejected as a satisfactory method of limiting profits in industry and commerce, as their effectiveness is uneven and they have a distorting effect on production and wages. 'What must be done is to maintain such a general level of purchasing power as does not allow of large profit margins or—to put it differently—which does not allow wage increases to be foisted into prices.'[2]

The LO recognizes that the curbing of the level of demand by fiscal and monetary policies may well create 'islands of unemployment'. If there were no rigidities in the economy and all the factors were completely mobile and responsive to the most subtle pressures of the market it would be possible so to control the aggregate level of demand that the amount of frictional unemployment would be minimal. Since this is not the case, the aggregate level of effective demand has to be boosted to an inflationary level to secure brimful employment. The policy the LO would like to see pursued is one focused on removing the 'islands of unemployment', rather than on raising the general level of effective demand. As it sees the problem, the LO suggests that the measures which might be taken would include public works, subsidies to individual firms and the placing of State orders with firms in localities where otherwise unemployment would be significant. Efforts should be made to encourage the voluntary transfer of labour to firms, trades and localities where the prospects of expansion are favourable, and much greater attention should be paid to the incentives to transfer. These ends might be attained by using revenue from anti-inflation budgets to finance comprehensive schemes aimed at removing any incipient unemployment and providing an incentive to transfer.

The main emphasis of the LO in this remarkably forthright and courageous attempt to grapple with the problem of inflation, is placed on the Budget as a counter-inflationary device. This arises from the distrust felt by the economic adviser of the LO of classical monetary policy, because of its association in the 1920's with deflation and unemployment. It is also due to a strong political objection to dear money. The managing director of the Svenska Handelsbanken, in his address given to the general meeting of the shareholders of the Bank in March 1952, remarked, after analysing the causes of the Swedish

[1] *Trade Unions and Full Employment.*
[2] *Ibid.*

inflation, that 'it must be admitted that a departure from cheap money appears to be a political impossibility in our country'. Subsequent events have shown, however, that the rate of interest must be allowed to rise if the supply of money is to be effectively curtailed.

The main reason for the change in attitude is that it has in practice proved to be more difficult than was imagined to use the Budget as an effective regulator of the economic system. Government expenditure has been one of the principal sources of inflation in Sweden; only twice since the war has a true budget surplus been attained. In theory there should be no difficulty in preventing budget deficits when employment is full and revenue is buoyant. In practice, however, it is frequently politically difficult to trim expenditure or raise taxes to the level necessary to maintain economic stability. It has now been realized by many supporters of the line of policy which called for cheap money and the use of the Budget as a stabilizer that this method has limited virtues. If the Budget is to do its job properly it must be supported by the right kind of monetary measures.

TABLE 10
Budget Balances
million Kronor

1946–1947	−210	1951–1952	+808
1947–1948	+92	1952–1953	−590
1948–1949	−181	1953–1954	−1,078
1949–1950	−427	1954–1955	−1,089
1950–1951	−198	1955–1956	−647

Sources: *Konjunkturjournalen. Statistisk Arsbok för Sverige*

The table opposite gives some indication of the extent to which the supply of money has increased in the post-war period. An expansion of this magnitude would not necessarily have been inflationary if there had been large supplies of idle labour available to put to work. But since employment was brimful, it was inevitable that wages would rise and it is not surprising that they rose much faster than production and thus inevitably drove up prices.

Attempts were made to check the expansion of credit as early as 1947, but the effect of the cheap money policy was to keep the market plentifully supplied with liquid funds. The fact that the rate of interest was fixed meant that the commercial banks could always rely upon the central bank to buy Government securities whenever they were put on the market. By this means the central bank made it possible for the commercial banks to meet the demand for credit and so to finance the inflationary rise in wages and prices which has taken place in Sweden.

A serious attempt was made in 1948 and 1949 to curtail the expansion of credit, but this was defeated by the Korean crisis, which brought a new wave of inflation. Voluntary credit restrictions were subsequently introduced, the commercial banks being asked to restrict their lending, but this did not have the desired result, since, for political reasons, the central bank was not able to take the supporting measures which were required, such as selling Government

TABLE 11

	Per cent Incease in Money Supply	Central Bank Discount Rate	Treasury Bills Held by Commercial Banks million kronor	Advances by Commercial and Savings Banks million kronor
1946	7	3.0	506	11,923
1947	5	3.0	152	13,358
1948	5	3.0	246	13,767
1949	3	3.0	490	14,462
1950	7	3.0	591	16,234
1951	22	3.0	899	17,516
1952	2	3.0	1,062	17,782
1953	5	2.75	1,437	18,494
1954	2	2.75	1,512	20,316
1955	1	3.75	699	20,273
1956	7	4.0	667	21,007
1957	5	5.0	—	—

Sources: *International Financial Statistics—IMF. Konjunkturjournalen*

securities. Thus, the commercial banks, which had been provided with the necessary means for a credit expansion, were not able to refuse to finance the great wage expansion of 1951. This pattern of events was repeated in 1953 and 1954 after the credit expansion had been temporarily checked in 1952. But then the climate began to change, partly because there was more resistance to inflation at home, and partly because of a growing resistance abroad. This change was reflected in the autumn of 1954, when it was felt to be necessary to set the rate of interest on a Government loan at four per cent to assure its success. This was a straw in the wind; by July 1957 the yield on Government bonds had risen to over four and a half per cent and the discount rate of the central bank had been pushed up to five per cent. Money, if not exactly dear by erstwhile standards, was no longer to be had at a bargain basement price.

Thus, after a decade of experiment with cheap money, the Swedes seem to have decided that under full employment inflation cannot be prevented without recourse to the traditional instrument of credit control and rationing. Whether or not they will succeed in maintaining unemployment at a level of about only two per cent, without price inflation, will depend not only on whether they can develop a more flexible monetary policy, but also on many other factors.

G

If the trade unions insist on advancing wages at a pace that far exceeds production, they will either promote an increase in unemployment or a breakdown in the tighter monetary policy, unless some way can be found to increase and then neutralize the flow of savings.

Increasing emphasis is being placed on the importance of savings as the source of new capital and as a counter-inflationary balance to the creation of additional purchasing power. A suggestion has been made that there should be some form of forced savings, but this notion has not had an enthusiastic reception. Nor has the proposal that instead of taking as much as possible out of industry in the form of money wages, a proportion should be 'ploughed back' into the capital of the enterprise and in return the workers, through their unions, should be given a share in management. In other words, there should be established schemes of co-partnership in place of the present system of industrial relations, which is based on the principle of autonomous parties to the collective agreement. It is not likely, however, that the Swedish unions would accept co-determination in place of the right to press for wage increases, as to some extent the German trade unions appear to have done.

Perhaps of much greater significance from the point of view of the supply of long-term savings are the proposals relating to the development of retirement pensions which were decided by referendum in 1957. The scheme, as proposed by the Social-Democrats, would, like the Labour Party's proposals for national superannuation in Britain, involve the accumulation of a massive fund financed to a large extent by employers' contributions. How, exactly, this scheme would affect economic activity it is extremely difficult to say.[1] It is widely believed that the scheme would lead to an increase in net saving and therefore be disinflationary. It is, however, impossible to be certain that this would be the result, since no one can predict with confidence what the future pattern of savings will be, if the scheme is put into practice.[2] It cannot, therefore, be taken for granted that the scheme will necessarily be non-inflationary in its consequence. Nor is it certain that it would make the task of preventing wages, salaries and profits from outstripping production any easier than it has been in the past.

The total of the fund estimated to have accrued by 1990 would amount to roughly five times the amount of capital now advanced by Swedish banks for investment. But if bank-provided funds rose by the same rate as during the past decade, they would be five times greater

---

[1] For discussion of the extreme difficulties which beset calculations of the effect of a scheme of this kind, see A. T. Peacock, 'The Economics of National Superannuation', *Three Banks Review*, September 1957.

[2] See Peacock, *op. cit.*

than the pension fund. However, bank advances are not likely to rise by such an amount if the fund comes into existence; and on any assumption the pension fund would become an important source of capital. The board of trustees appointed to administer the fund would, therefore, be an extremely influential body; it could profoundly alter the control of the flow of investment funds and, therefore, of the future pattern of industrial and social development. In this respect a new element in the dimensions of financial control is introduced. Whether this would lead to a more democratic control of economic policy, as is thought by supporters of the scheme, remains an open question. It could result in a weakening of the authority of the Government in the economic field, and thus make more difficult the task of maintaining a balanced economic growth.

The lessons of Swedish experience would seem to suggest that the centralization of wage bargaining, under the aegis of a powerful Trades Union Congress and Employers' Confederation, is not in itself any guarantee that wages will not rise in response to the level of aggregate demand. Although the central organization of the Swedish trade unions has continued to pursue a national wages policy it has recognized that the main responsibility for preventing inflation must rest with the Government. Indeed it has stated that inflation is inevitable if the level of demand is allowed to rise to a point where there are more jobs available than there are men and women to fill them. It remains yet to be seen whether the Swedish labour movement, political as well as industrial, is prepared to accept the practical implications of the conclusions accepted on the analytical plane.

CHAPTER 7

Wage Policy in Australia: the Arbitration System

No country has had a longer experience than Australia of settling wages by governmental regulation. It is now over half a century since the Commonwealth Court of Conciliation and Arbitration was established, and this was antedated in the State of Victoria, which eight years earlier, in 1896, had set up a Wages Board. The advantages of deciding wage levels by an independent body with legal powers seemed so strong to the majority of Australians that by 1912 each state, some of them after considerable experiment, had adopted the principle in one form or another.[1]

The fact that the Federal Government has only limited powers over economic affairs and that in important respects each state may determine the policy to be pursued within its own borders, has produced a machinery for the regulation of wages and other aspects of industrial relations that is highly complex.[2] The Commonwealth Court of Arbitration is, however, the most important of the wage fixing bodies in the galaxy, and since it is the sun round which the others cluster, they feel the power of its radiation. The awards of the Commonwealth Court directly cover some forty per cent of all Australian workers, but in several states Wages Boards and Arbitration Courts are obliged by state legislation to incorporate in their own awards federal standards established by the Commonwealth Court. The basic wage, which is determined by the Commonwealth Court and other industrial tribunals, accounts, according to one authority, for some eighty-five per cent of the average total wage received by an Australian worker.[3] This figure is likely to be subject to change, but since the differentials for skill and responsibility are also determined to a major extent by statutory bodies it establishes the extent to which wage movements in Australia may be

[1] O. de Foenander, *Towards Industrial Peace in Australia* (1937).
[2] A description of the arbitration machinery is given by Kenneth F. Walker in his excellent study *Industrial Relations in Australia* (1956).
[3] D. W. Oxnam, 'Industrial Arbitration in Australia: its Effects on Wages and Unions', *Industrial and Labour Relations Review*, July 1956.

affected by decisions of the Commonwealth Court and state tribunals.

In its origins, compulsory arbitration was desired as a means of (a) preventing industrial disputes, (b) protecting the interests of the community, (c) bringing about a fairer distribution of income from industry, (d) improving the organization of workpeople.[1] The notion that the Court should accept as one of its responsibilities the promotion of economic growth and the maintenance of economic stability only came up much later as a consequence of events in the inter-war period.

Compulsory arbitration has undoubtedly contributed to the growth and strength of Australian trade unionism. Today, more than sixty per cent of the total number of employees are to be found in trade unions. Whether the effect of compulsory arbitration on the character of trade unionism in Australia has been entirely good is a matter that is open to dispute, but no objective examination of the government, administration and policy of labour organizations could fail to note the strength of the bureaucratic, irresponsible element in their make-up.

In every other respect compulsory arbitration seems to have been of an even more dubious advantage. It has failed to provide Australia with the peaceful industrial relations its advocates confidently expected it to produce. Few other countries can show as bad a record of strikes as Australia, and some authorities attribute this fact to the system of compulsory arbitration which, they claim, exacerbates relations between employers and employed.[2]

Whether the cause of Australia's poor standard of industrial relations is to be found in the system of compulsory arbitration is a matter for controversy; so too is the effect of compulsory arbitration on wage movements. But in the light of Australia's economic difficulties during the past forty years it could hardly be claimed by the most fervent admirer of compulsory arbitration that as an instrument of economic control it had been a tremendous success. The negative argument that without it things might have been very much worse is, of course, not subject to test, and is, therefore, simply a matter of opinion. Since, however, the Commonwealth Arbitration Court has 'evolved into a major agent of economic decision making, and consciously bases its important decisions on economic grounds'[3] its record in this respect will be examined at greater length.

[1] K. F. Walker, op. cit.
[2] E. P. Kelsall, 'Compulsory Arbitration and Industrial Conflict in Australia'. An unpublished PhD Thesis in the University of London.
[3] K. F. Walker, op. cit.

The Early Objectives of the Court

The father of the Australian arbitration system was Mr Justice Higgins. It was he who, in 1904, drafted the original Act which established the Commonwealth Court of Conciliation and Arbitration. Higgins was concerned to see that the principles of law should apply to the settlement of disputes in industry as in other spheres of human conflict. He believed, as do some people today, that industrial relations ought not to be conducted on the basis of negotiation from strength, with the attendant danger of strike or lockout, but should be regulated according to notions of justice set forth in Common Rules established by the Court. In this way, it would, he believed, be possible to determine fair wages and working conditions on a national basis and so avoid resort to industrial strife.[1] As President of the Arbitration Court from 1906 until 1920 Higgins was able to promulgate his ideas in the awards that he gave. His most famous decision, which laid the foundation of the Court's policy on wages for the next quarter of a century, was made in the so-called Harvester case in 1907.

The Harvester award established a basic minimum wage, which was set at a level which in the opinion of Mr Justice Higgins would meet 'the normal needs of the average employee regarded as a human being in a civilized community . . .'. The average employee that Mr Justice Higgins had in mind was assumed to be a married man with a family of three children.[2] In 1912 an index of the cost of living was published for the first time, and in the following year the policy of providing a basic minimum real wage to which every person at work was entitled was taken a stage further by a decision to make an annual revision in the light of changes in the index.

In addition to the basic wage, the Commonwealth Court was faced with the problem of fixing appropriate margins for skill and responsibility. This task is an extremely difficult one to perform satisfactorily and the Court may have inhibited the development of sound wage structures.

Wage Policy in the Slump

In 1921 the basic wage was raised by three shillings and made auto-

---

[1] See N. Palmer, *Henry Bournes Higgins* (1931).

[2] There was very little statistical basis for the adoption of a family unit of this size, or for the estimate of the wage that would keep such a family in frugal comfort. Mr Justice Higgins based his decision on the examination of nine household budgets and the statements of a few estate agents. Thirteen years later a Royal Commission on the basic wage discovered that Australian industries were, in effect, paying for 450,000 non-existent wives and over 2,000,000 non-existent children. B. H. Higgins, 'Wage Fixing by Compulsory Arbitration', *Social Research*, September 1951.

matically adjustable at quarterly intervals. The next revision of the basic wage came in 1931, but this time it was in a downward direction. The basic wage in money terms had been falling with the price index during 1930 but the employers and many economists were of the opinion that this was not enough to bring about an economic recovery. After hearings lasting two months the Commonwealth Arbitration Court decided in favour of cutting the basic money wage by a further ten per cent. The Court was convinced that this step would lead to higher profits, a rise in investment and an increase in employment, ultimately leading to a rise in the national income and aggregate wages. In particular it was believed that this step would help 'to spread the burden' and provide much needed assistance to the primary producers.

Opinion is divided as to whether the drastic reduction in the basic wage helped Australia to weather the great depression of the 'thirties. Since real wages hardly fell at all it did not cause any great suffering to the workers in employment; it did, however, help to relieve the pressure on the export industries and it did encourage home industries. It has been concluded by one distinguished authority, that 'the policy adopted by the Federal Court was substantially correct and made a big contribution to recovery'.[1] However, the same writer is extremely critical of the theoretical analyses on which the judges based their decision, and their uncritical acceptance of statistics of doubtful accuracy. The cut in money wages was significant because it allowed prices to fall, and so relieved the burden that had been thrown on the farmers by the fall in export demand. The Court's reasoning implied that internal prices would not fall, but had they not done so, the farmers would have suffered much more. The Court must, however, in the opinion of Reddaway, be given credit for recognizing the importance of an exchange depreciation and a policy of monetary expansion, in addition to the wage cuts. These policies could not, however, pull Australia out of the slump into which the whole world had plunged. No country as dependent on exports as Australia could, acting alone, spend itself out of a slump. It might, by judicious monetary and fiscal policies, maintain employment at a higher level than would otherwise be the case, but a severe adverse shift in the terms of trade and a fall in the demand for exports must involve a fall in real consumption. The Court was, therefore, entirely correct to reject the arguments put forward by the trade unions that the slump could be overcome without making any adjustments to wages, since, in the circumstances, the only alternative, a

[1] See W. B. Reddaway, 'Australian Wage Policy, 1929–1937', *International Labour Review*. March 1938.

further and even more severe devaluation of the Australian pound, was not really politically feasible, though it might have been used to a greater extent. Such a policy would not have shielded the workers from the impact of the fall in demand for Australian exports, which was the crux of the problem.

Gradually the moderate depreciation of the Australian pound, the recovery in the price of Australian exports as world prices began to rise, and the increased expenditure on public investment, contributed to an improvement in the state of economic prosperity which by 1934 had become significant. Unemployment among trade unionists, which had reached the record level of 28.7 per cent in 1931–32, had fallen to 18.9 per cent in 1934–35.[1] In the light of this recovery the Commonwealth Arbitration Court was persuaded in 1934 that it was safe to restore, at least nominally, the ten per cent cut in the basic wage which it had made in 1931. The Court also decided to break with the previous basis upon which it had calculated the basic wage. Henceforth, the 'capacity to pay' which had, of course, been the underlying factor in the 1931 cut in the basic wage, would be the principal criterion followed by the Court. This principle, however, would not be applied to single firms or even industries, but to the economy as a whole. The notion that the basic wage should be in some way linked to a concept of need was not, however, entirely repudiated, and still lingers to the present day.

A Policy for Prosperity

In 1937 it was judged by the Commonwealth Arbitration Court that a 'prosperity loading' which had been granted by each of the six states could be added on to the basic wage so as to bring it, in real terms, to the level which prevailed in 1929. In arriving at this decision the Court was guided for the most part by the submissions of Mr W. B. Reddaway, who had been called as an independent expert witness. The Court accepted Reddaway's contention that a substantial increase in wages was justified by the restoration of prosperity, and by the rise in export prices and home investment.[2] Reddaway had further suggested that the size of the wage increase recommended could also be justified on the grounds that it would prevent an over-rapid expansion of demand, based upon profit expectations. The wage increase, by pushing up costs, was, therefore, looked upon by Reddaway as having a deflationary effect. By a well-timed wage increase, if the calculations were right, economic progress could be

[1] *Monthly Review of Business Statistics.*
[2] See Reddaway, p. 326, *op. cit.*

kept on a steady path instead of moving in fits and starts.[1] This argument was based upon the assumption that the increase in wage costs could not be passed on in higher prices without having a bad effect on capital expenditure and exports; it was also assumed that the higher cost structure would not be 'floated off' on an expansion of bank credit.

The Court clearly found the economic reasoning difficult to follow even though it accepted the thesis put to it, and made up its mind that it ought to increase wages. As the Court saw the problem, wage increases could be inflationary or deflationary and it was obviously not certain what the consequences of its action would be. 'If at any time,' stated the judgment, 'it is made to appear that the capitalist section for other reasons than an excessively high level of wages then prevailing, is refraining from investing "savings" in its control, it may be quite good policy to raise the wage level so as to transfer the spending power from it to the wage earner section. It does not appear to be suggested that this is the position at present in the Commonwealth. But it is conceivable that such a position may exist at some time in a country, while at another time in the same country *entrepreneurs* may be showing a tendency to invest "savings" to an excessive extent in producer goods and thus to lead up to a boom and subsequent slump. The two conditions tend to be alternative, both of them largely due to prevailing states of mind. In either case a raising of the wage level may be indicated as a remedy, but obviously no economic physician can prescribe with precision the proper amount of the dose.'

Whatever the degree of uncertainty in the mind of the Court when they arrived at their decision the dose was apparently about right, since it had no very serious repercussions so far as can be discerned. Unemployment remained at about nine per cent of trade union membership, investment tended to increase, production rose and the real wage went up. The unions were in the process of seeking a further increase in the basic wage when the second World War started. In view of the seriousness of the situation they decided to postpone their application until a more propitious moment. In 1940 a general economic stabilization programme was introduced; regulations were introduced as a temporary wartime measure to make award rates, in certain cases, maxima as well as minima. The cost of living was held down from 1943, by special measures, including subsidies and price controls, and, since wages were pegged to a price index, they too were held in reasonable check by comparison with Britain and America.

[1] See Reddaway, p. 326, *op. cit.*

The £10 a Week Basic Wage

At the end of the war the unions sought to secure a reduction in the standard hours of work from forty-four to forty and in interim adjustment in the basic wage. The Court fairly speedily made an increase of about seven per cent, but it took over twelve months to decide to reduce the standard working week to forty hours as desired by the unions.

Criticism of the Arbitration Court had tended to grow during the war and it was reinforced when the Court took so long to hear and decide the *Forty Hours Case*.[1] The Government, fearing that the Court would not be able to cope with the pressure of cases, and wishing to encourage more autonomous agreements between unions and employers, decided in 1947 to reorganize the system. A Conciliation Commission was established, with power to seek solutions to disputes by way of persuasion, and to make binding awards on such issues as 'margins', piece rates and working conditions. The Court was still, however, to remain at the heart of the compulsory arbitration system, which in its essence remained unchanged, and in particular the Court would still be responsible for determining the basic wage and the length of the standard week.

The Court was called upon to discharge its basic function when, in 1949, a number of unions asked for a revision of the basic wage. The Australian Council of Trade Unions sought to persuade the Court to raise the basic wage to a minimum of £10 per week; an increase of over sixty per cent in the wages of men and considerably more for women. The unions claimed that they were entitled to an increase in the basic wage on several grounds. They argued that an increase in the basic wage was due because the productive capacity of the nation had grown. The economy could sustain an increase in the basic wage which would 'give to and maintain for a family of five (a man, wife and three dependent children) a standard of living which is the highest possible as a national minimum consistent with modern living standards and the productive capacity of the nation'.[2] It was further argued by the unions that the standard of living made possible by the basic wage had actually fallen since before the war; this was due to the inadequacy of the retail price index, to which the wage was geared, which failed to measure the real change in the cost of living. Another ground on which the claim was based was the shift in the distribution of the national income, brought about by the great pros-

[1] See O. de R. Foenander, 'The Forty Hours Case and the Change in Standard Hours in Australian Industry'. *International Labour Review*, December 1948.

[2] Quoted by J. E. Isaac, 'The Claim for a £10 Basic Wage in Australia', *International Labour Review*, February 1951.

perity of the farmers, who were enjoying a fabulous export boom in wool and other agricultural products, which had resulted in a fall in the share of total incomes going to labour.

The Court, after a careful examination of the facts, found that real weekly wage rates had risen since 1939. After the Acting Commonwealth Statistician had fully explained the strength and weakness of the retail price index in use, as a measuring instrument of changes in retail prices, the Court rejected this basis of the union's claim as ill-founded. Expert witnesses from both sides were heard by the Court on the alleged unfavourable shift in the distribution of income. In this clash of opinion the facts were obscured by the limitations of Australian statistics, but the employers' expert on balance seems to have had the better of the argument on technical grounds, and the Court found that the unions' case was unproved.[1] The probable truth was that there had been a substantial shift of income in favour of the farmers, but that at this stage wage earners had not been left behind; the section of the community which had suffered was that which lived on rents, pensions and salaries.

The Court was still faced, however, by the fundamental question as to whether the basic wage should be raised on the egalitarian principle, followed by the Court since the Harvester award, that the economy could sustain the payment of a higher wage to those on the minimum scale.

On this basic issue the Court was divided. The Chief Judge took the view that it was the duty of the Court to say what level of wage would be 'just and reasonable for an adult male or female, as the case may be, with reference to what it finds to be the expenditure which will be necessary to purchase what it regards as an appropriate standard of living for him or her'.[2] He went on to say that in arriving at this standard the Court would be influenced by the capacity of the economy to sustain the level it thought desirable to set. The Chief Judge was extremely conscious of the dangers of inflation and he was clearly moved by the fact that there had recently been a seven per cent increase in the basic wage, and a ten per cent reduction in the standard weekly hours of work. Wages and prices, as Table 12 shows, had been rising swiftly and the Chief Judge emphasized that failure to arrest this trend would endanger Australia's unbalanced economy and threaten a large number of people with poverty. In the circumstances he was not prepared to take any risks and he rejected the unions' claim on these grounds.

The Chief Judge's two colleagues took rather a different view of

[1] See J. E. Isaac, *op. cit.*
[2] Quoted by J. E. Isaac, *op. cit.*

TABLE 12

	Wage Rates[1]	Earnings	Prices[1]		Volume of Money[2]
				1945	100
1945–46	100	100	100		
				1946	112
1946–47	106	104	102		
				1947	114
1947–48	117	116	109		
				1948	120
1948–49	131	132	120		
				1949	131
1949–50	142	145	130		
				1950	153
1950–51	171	174	158		
				1951	180
1951–52	209	215	183		
				1952	179
1952–53	231	235	199		
				1953	195
1953–54	239	246	205		
				1954	214
1954–55	242	257	207		
				1955	222
1955–56	250	274	214		
				1956	224

Sources: [1] *Monthly Review of Business Statistics*
[2] *Commonwealth Bank Annual Reports*

the situation. All three agreed that wages and prices were intimately linked, but Mr Justice Foster departed from the Chief Judge in his assessment of the responsibility of the Court. He thought that it was possible that an increase in the basic wage would be followed by the unions seeking to raise the whole complex of wage rates, *pari passu*, but that this was not for the Court to consider. The problem of controlling inflation was not fundamentally a matter within the competence of the Court, but was a duty which fell to the Government.

Mr Justice Foster, therefore, decided to support an increase in the basic wage of £1 per week; this was a rise of approximately fifteen per cent, as against the original claim which amounted to sixty per cent. He arrived at this figure from the fact that wage statistics showed that average industrial earnings were roughly £1 per week above the average level of rates that had been awarded by the Arbitration Courts and Wages Boards. Since the fact that these wages were actually being paid demonstrated that the economy could bear this load, it was not unreasonable to conclude that the economy could sustain the consolidation of the higher level of earnings brought about by the competition for labour. Mr Justice Foster stated that 'the Court must, as in the past, go on assuming that its awards will be observed as maximums as well as minimums, and to refuse to contemplate or to take responsibility for what employers individually or as organizations may do. We can merely tell them that the Court has awarded what it regards as fair, equitable and reasonable and in the public interest. If it is disregarded and there is substituted for the Court's judgment one of their own making the Court can do nothing whatever about it.'[1]

Mr Justice Dunphy was also of the opinion that it was safe to raise the basic wage by £1 per week; thus by a majority of two to one the Court found in favour of this course. The controversy as to whether the effect of the increase would be inflationary was quickly settled, since prices were twenty-four per cent higher in 1951 than they had been in 1950, wages having risen, including the rise in the basic wage, by twenty-five per cent in the same period. Blame for the rise in prices could not be entirely placed on the trade unions, since the price obtained for Australian exports continued to soar until the middle of 1951. The extraordinary level of external demand inevitably pulled up with it the prices of agricultural products sold upon the domestic market. The prices of manufactured goods also rose, since they were influenced by the rise in wages induced by the rise in the cost of living, and by the pressure of demand generated by farmers who had money to spend and did so with abandon.

Automatic Cost of Living Adjustments Abandoned
The unions continued to press for higher wages and shorter hours. In October 1951 the metal trades employers sought to counter the demand of the unions for increased margins for skill and responsibility by asking the Court to increase the standard working week from forty to forty-four hours. The unions countered with an irresponsible claim for a reduction of standard hours to thirty per week.[2] The claim of the metal trades for wider margins was dismissed by the Conciliation Commission in January 1952. There was considerable substance in the claim, since the differentials for skill and responsibility had been steadily narrowed by the continued cost of living increases in the basic wage. The Commissioner argued, however, that in the circumstances an increase in the margins would be inflationary; he considered that the public interest demanded that he should not make an

[1] Quoted by J. E. Isaac, *op. cit.*

[2] Irresponsible claims and counter-claims are not made solely by the unions; employers are just as ready as the unions to make demands that no reasonable person would expect to see met. This type of behaviour does not encourage good industrial relations, but it seems to be an inevitable feature of a compulsory arbitration system. Recent developments in the arbitration system may, by reducing the influence of the Court, alter the attitude of both employers and unions.

award that would simply be followed by a claim for an increase in the basic wage.[1]

In the meantime, the economic situation had undergone a change. Export prices were no longer rising; imports, which had increased as a result of the strong home demand, far exceeded the value of Australian export earnings, which fell by one-third in twelve months, with the inevitable consequence of a large balance of payments deficit. Thus overflowing employment in which vacancies far outnumbered the workers available gave way to an increase in unemployment which reached roughly three per cent early in 1953. It was the employers' contention that Australia had priced herself out of world markets and that it was essential to reduce costs to restore the situation. They therefore asked the Court for (1) a reduction in the basic wage; (2) a reduction in the basic wage for women from seventy-five to sixty per cent of the men's rate; (3) an increase in the standard hours of work from forty to forty-four; and (4) the abolition of the system of adjusting the basic wage automatically to changes in the retail price index.

The Court eventually decided to reject each of these demands with the exception of the fourth. The application for the suspension of the automatic adjustment of the basic wage to changes in the retail price index was granted, because the Court had come to the conclusion that the basic wage should be founded on the capacity of the economy to pay the highest wage possible, rather than on the principle of minimum needs. Since there was no ground for assuming that the capacity of the economy to sustain the level of the basic wage would vary with changes in the cost of living, there was no longer any reason to maintain the link between the wage level and the price index. The Court also held that the automatic adjustment of wages with prices had contributed to the inflationary pressure. It further accepted the employers' view that the frequency of wage changes created difficulties for business undertakings.[2]

In arriving at its decision the Court intimated that in future it would have regard to the 'total industry of the country in assessing the capacity of the community to pay a foundation wage'.[3] It advised parties to future cases to 'direct their attention to the broader aspects of the economy, such as are indicated by a study of the following matters: employment; investment; production and productivity; overseas trade; overseas balances; the competitive position of

[1] J. E. Isaac, 'The Basic Wage and Standard Hours Inquiry in Australia, 1952–53', *International Labour Review*, June 1954.
[2] See J. E. Isaac, *op. cit.*
[3] 77 C.A.R.

secondary industry, and retail trade'.[1] There could thus be no doubt that the Court had finally come to see itself not as setting a minimum wage based on the basic needs, but as setting a 'foundation wage' based upon the economic capacity of the nation.

The decision of the Commonwealth Court did not prevent the six states from continuing to tie basic wages to the cost of living if they so desired. Labour Governments in Victoria and New South Wales legislated to oblige their wage regulating agencies to maintain the system of automatic adjustments; and the Queensland Industrial Court continued to make quarterly changes. The effect of the decision of the Commonwealth Court of Arbitration was thus not felt as sharply as it would otherwise have been.

Arbitration Awards: Inflationary or Deflationary?
The decision of the Court naturally aroused considerable opposition from the trade unions, but there were also a number of professional economists who believed that the automatic cost of living adjustments had not been inflationary. Kingsley Laffer, for example, argued that 'in the absence of effective fiscal, monetary and other measures to check excess demand, the cost of living adjustments appear to have served a useful deflationary purpose'.[2]

Laffer was of the opinion that the rise in wage costs checked the over-rapid development of home industries that occurred in the post-war boom. 'The potential competition from lower cost imports has put a strong brake on further investment in these industries. Apart from this, the rise in wages and prices has helped to create a shortage of working capital, which has assisted the monetary authorities to check excess demand. As the cost of living adjustments have been a major factor in the development of these deflationary effects, their economic importance has been great.'[3]

The deflationary effects of the wage increases granted by the Courts prior to 1951 were probably not as great as Laffer suggests. So long as the wage increases could be passed on in the form of higher prices without any fall in demand, and the rapid and continuous rise is clear evidence that there was no significant fall in aggregate demand, then they were not having much disinflationary effect. It is true that the Australian inflation was fed from outside in the form of export income, which in turn led to a great expansion of bank credit. It was inevitable that prices and wages should rise internally and that

[1] 77 C.A.R.

[2] Kingsley Laffer, 'Cost of Living Adjustments in Australian Wage Determination', *Industrial and Labour Relations Review*, January 1954.

[3] Kingsley Laffer, *op. cit.*

imports should be attracted when the volume of money rose by six per cent in 1947–48, ten per cent in 1948–49, sixteen per cent in 1949–50, and no less than nineteen per cent in 1950–51.[1] To check the mounting inflation the Commonwealth Government increased taxes, budgeted for a surplus and tightened the control of capital issues. This policy was supported by the Central Bank, which limited the expansion of advances and controlled the liquid reserves of the trading banks, though not very successfully, until the tremendous fall in export receipts and rise in imports drove up the rate of interest and led to a shortage of liquid funds. The main weakness in the monetary policy of the authorities was that they were reluctant to allow the rate of interest to rise and to prevent this from happening supported the market, thus increasing the supply and demand for funds and rendering the policy of restricting the volume of new money less effective.

Laffer is convinced that the cost of living wage adjustments actually helped the Commonwealth Government to adopt anti-inflation measures, simply because they focused attention on the problem. Paradoxical as that argument might sound, Laffer is certainly on strong ground in pointing out that the Government's anti-inflationary measures, introduced in the latter half of 1951, helped to check the price inflation and so reduced the cost of living adjustments to moderate size. 'There is no doubt,' he writes, 'that the Government was right to direct its main attention to demand inflation. Cost inflation helped to check demand inflation. If, however, cost inflation had been checked but not demand inflation, the result would have been to accentuate the latter. The checking of demand inflation, on the other hand, helped to check cost inflation as well.'[2]

An argument in favour of compulsory arbitration, which is based upon the notion that wages must be raised in order to curb demand inflation, as previously noted, is too subtle to be easily appreciated and it is perhaps not surprising that Laffer's opinions were not those of the Commonwealth Court when it made its decision to abandon quarterly wage adjustments. A more powerful argument in favour of the Court's decision was made by Laffer himself. He admits that in circumstances of rising import prices and falling export prices, there would be a rise in home costs, brought about by the tying of wages to prices. This could only lead to a balance of payments crisis and the eventual depreciation of the Australian pound if the situation were not corrected. The linking of wages to the cost of living inevitably introduces an element of rigidity into any economy which may

[1] *Commonwealth Bank Annual Reports.*
[2] Kingsley Laffer, *op. cit.*

produce results that are exactly the opposite of those sought by trade union leaders. If only short-run money and real wages are the goal of the unions then they are bound to endanger the long-run prosperity of their members.

The problem of economic control becomes extremely complex when a country's economy has a highly important agricultural section, which is also the principal earner of foreign currency. When export income rises the farmers are prosperous and farm wages rise; the demand generated leads to a rise in the price of goods and services purchased by the farm community; the increase in the cost of living leads fairly rapidly to wage advances, when wages are linked to the price index and are automatically adjusted at quarterly intervals. The rise in industrial wages further adds to industrial costs and to the pressure of demand; home produced consumer goods rise again in price and at the same time as this process is going on, the buoyant level of home demand induces a rapid increase in the flow of imports. The next stage arrives when the import bill exceeds the receipts from exports and a balance of payments crisis occurs. The authorities then seek to cut down imports by restrictions and tariffs, to curb home-generated demand by budgeting for a surplus and by monetary policy.

In the sequence of events outlined above wage policy plays an important, but relatively secondary role. However, the evolution of the thinking of the Court in relation to the problem of economic stability as seen by judgments in 1956 and 1957 is, in the light of previous policy, of great interest. It is now quite clear that the Court takes the view that to tie wages to the cost of living is a mistake. In rejecting an application from the unions, in 1956, for the restoration of the quarterly automatic adjustments to the basic wage in the light of changes in the 'C' series price index, the Court underlined its reasons for departing from that long-established practice. It re-emphasized that there could be no basis for assuming that the capacity of the economy to sustain a basic wage could be determined simply by changes in a price index. The Court, indeed, went a stage further because it asserted that reference to the 'C' series index, or to the new interim price index, would not be of any use, since neither index could accurately measure changes in the cost of living. By implication, the Court was saying that it now completely rejected the notion that there was any standard of real wage that it could determine irrespective of other economic conditions. The act of linking basic money wage rates to any index of price changes was, therefore, only likely to mislead and might have grave disadvantages.

The Court finally came to its decision in 1956, raising the basic

H

wage by 10*s*, and in 1957 the Commission, following a similar application, again made the same award. They did so after a full review of the factors which, in 1953, the Court had stated should be taken into account. The Court, in its 1956 judgment, was particularly concerned with the relation between wage increases and the stimulation of further inflation, and it only arrived at its decision after lengthy analysis of the economic situation. It is apparent that the Court was not quite certain of the consequences of its decision, but it came to the conclusion that, in spite of the dangers, the basic wage should be increased. A year later the Commission concluded that the inflationary danger had receded, but it then seemed to argue, somewhat perversely, in the light of the previous judgment, that it would ignore the effect of its decision on demand inflation. 'Although the influence of the supply of money even when directly affected by increase of funds overseas is of paramount importance, it is controlled by governmental and banking policy. There is nothing to suggest to this Commission that the wage increase to be prescribed cannot be accommodated within that policy. The problem of inflation needs no further mention.'[1] The problem of inflation, though dismissed in this peremptory fashion, was given further consideration. The Commission admitted that the award would raise spending power by £30 million and that this would have a tendency to raise prices. But 'while attention has been paid to this fact and some hesitation caused because of it the conclusion reached is that it is in the best interests of the whole community and constitutes industrial justice that the worker under federal awards should receive an increase of 10s in his basic wage'.[2]

The refusal of the Arbitration Court to adjust the basic wage to the cost of living is not, as the Court seems to assume, likely to prevent wage incomes from rising. Indeed there is evidence that average earnings have risen considerably more than wage rates in the period since 1938. At the time of the rigorous wage freeze, during the war, earnings in manufacturing industry rose to forty-one per cent above the pre-war level, whereas wage rates in manufacturing industry were up by only twenty-four per cent. From 1945 until 1951 wage rates and earnings moved very closely together. Since 1951 and the abolition of the automatic quarterly adjustments to the basic wage, earnings have tended to draw away from wage rates, as will be seen from Table 12. It would thus appear that wages are being pulled up by a demand generated by inflation. In other words, it would seem, on the

[1] Commonwealth Conciliation and Arbitration Commission Basic Wage Judgment 1957.
[2] *Op. cit.*

evidence of wage movements since 1938, that, by and large, the changes in wage rates had been caused by price movements exogenously determined.

It would appear not unreasonable to conclude that it is not, therefore, possible to control the Australian inflation by means of a wage policy administered by the Commonwealth Arbitration Court, since the Court could not prevent an employer from paying above its awards. Furthermore, the trend of the arbitration system, in the post-war years, has been away from the administrative control of wages, implicit in the doctrine of Mr Justice Higgins, the father of the system, to a state of greater autonomy.[1] The development, in 1947, of the arbitration system, so as to provide for Conciliation Commissioners with a special responsibility for encouraging employers and unions to arrive at agreements without the intervention of the Arbitration Court was an important step in the direction of promoting more private settlements and less public control. Two subsequent revisions of the Act have given the Commissioners greater authority at the expense of the Commonwealth Arbitration Court. To what extent these changes are likely to bring about less reliance on the Arbitration Court it is difficult to say. It is necessary to remember, however, that wage changes are not the sole prerogative of the Commonwealth Court and Conciliation Commissioners. The separate states have their own machinery and can, to an important degree, follow their own policies.

There have been moves by Communist-led unions to persuade the Australian Council of Trade Unions to refuse to continue to support compulsory arbitration, but they have not been acceptable to the majority. Both those in favour of compulsory arbitration and those against expect more from a change than would, if the analysis presented is correct, be actually secured.

The arbitration system has lasted so long and is now deeply entrenched in Australia precisely because, by and large, it has produced decisions which have been acceptable to both sides of industry. These decisions have been acceptable because both sides have known that they were not very different from what would have been arrived at in the end, in the prevailing economic circumstances, by a market process of bargaining, and, it must be added, because if the award pressed too hard there were always ways and means of adjusting it.

The members of the Court have tried to accomplish much more than simply to find the market price for labour in given circumstances. They have sought to direct the course and pattern of wages in accord-

[1] See M. Perlman, *Judges in Industry: A Study of Labour Arbitration in Australia* (1954).

ance with their notions of social and economic needs. The difficulties which faced the Courts in their earliest days were analysed in great detail by George Anderson, who came to the conclusion thirty years ago that a body of lawyers were not particularly well equipped to resolve the acute conflicts of sectional interest, social justice and economic theories with which the Courts were confronted.[1] Recent investigations have shown that the Courts are no more able today to arrive with certainty at the solution to the problem they believe they are trying to resolve.[2] This is not, however, because the Courts are composed of lawyers, as Anderson and many other critics consider. The situation would be no better if, as is sometimes suggested, the Court had a staff of experts to provide its members with specialist advice. The Court can, and does, hear expert witnesses, but experts do not always agree, and they can be wrong. The real problem is that there are always honest differences of opinion which arise from differences of interest and analysis.

If the Courts were to ride roughshod over the interests of the parties with the purpose of imposing some point of view advised by experts, but not acceptable to the unions or employers, the problem of enforcement would soon become insuperable. The standard of rightness must, therefore, inevitably become not some theoretical notion, but what the situation makes possible. This is not to say that the Courts cannot exercise any influence; their decisions may very well help to push the course of events in one direction or another, but it is very unlikely that the Courts could, over the long run, effectively determine that wage levels should be quite different from those which the fundamental economic and social forces would in any case combine to produce.

Opinion in Australia is divided as to the extent to which wage increases have been the cause of inflation, and how far the Arbitration system has been culpable. Wherever the truth lies, and it would seem to lie on balance with those who hold that the decisions of the Courts have not been the main factor, there is little evidence that the Commonwealth Arbitration system will be any more able to prevent inflation in the future than it has been in the past. This is probably one of the reasons, among others, why there is a growing interest in monetary policy and in the correct techniques to be used to maintain full employment, economic growth and price stability.[3]

[1] George Anderson, *Fixation of Wages in Australia* (1929).

[2] B. H. Higgins, *Social Research*, September 1951.

[3] Cf. Dr H. C. Coombs, 'The Development of Monetary Policy in Australia,' English, Scottish and Australian Bank Research Lecture, University of Queensland, 1954.

The Australian Labour Party is still violently hostile to the use of higher interest rates and credit restriction as a means of controlling the economy. The Government is, in principle, in favour of using monetary policy as a main instrument to curb inflation, but the Commonwealth Bank has, so far, been extremely sensitive to political criticism and has proceeded with great caution. It is likely, however, especially if inflation is checked in other parts of the world, that Australia will, in fact, have to maintain a stricter control over the supply of money than has been the case in the recent past.

CHAPTER 8

Wage Policy in the Netherlands

The movement of wages has been centrally controlled in the Netherlands since the end of the Nazi occupation. Faced with a tremendous problem of reconstruction the Government, with the support of employers and trade unions, decided that it could not allow wages to find their own level. It feared that to return to the pre-war system of unrestricted collective bargaining would result in an inflationary spiral and, possibly, social unrest that would endanger national recovery.

The Foundation of Labour

In May 1945, it was announced that trade union and employers' organizations had formed a joint body to which they gave the name the Foundation of Labour. The roots of the Foundation of Labour stretched back to the aftermath of the first World War, when a Labour Board was set up to advise the Government. There were suggestions that employers and workers should enter into closer working relations, and in 1928 discussions on outstanding issues were begun between the employers and the three central trade union organizations, Catholic, Protestant and Socialist. This meeting produced no outstanding results, but it was followed by further conferences from time to time. During the second World War, under the unifying influence of alien occupation, the two sides agreed to establish a permanent body to deal with the formidable problems likely to arise during the reconstruction period. After the Foundation of Labour had been established it was quickly accepted by the Government as an advisory authority on industrial and social problems, and many of the advances in standards of employment during the past decade have emanated from the policies of the Foundation.

The Foundation of Labour is composed of an equal number of representatives of employers' organizations and trade unions, and it is assisted by independent experts. The interests of the Foundation embrace wages, social insurance, health and safety, productivity, technical training and employment. It does not include under its jurisdiction the broad issues of economic policy, though it cannot ignore factors that will inevitably affect the levels of employment, wages and prices. Thus, though its field of action is fairly clearly defined, there is no hard and fast limit beyond which it could not venture. An important consequence of the establishment of the Foundation has been the virtual transference of collective bargaining from the industrial to the national level. This development was facilitated in Holland by the structure of the trade union movement, which reflects the social divisions in the country. These run along religious lines, and in most industries and trades workers may belong to either Catholic, Protestant or secular[1] organizations. Thus there are three trade union federations, each of them firmly cemented together by deeply held religious or social principles, which cut across the occupational and industrial interests of wage and salary earners. In Britain the common vocational interests of workpeople are not subordinated to an ideological pattern of organization and this results in a far more powerful inclination towards industrial autonomy than is the case in Holland.

Even if trade unionists in Holland were all in one national federation they would not add up to as many members as the largest of the British trade unions. The Netherlands Federation of Labour (NVV) has approximately 500,000 members, the Catholic Workers' Movement (KAB) 350,000, and the Protestant Federation of Labour (CNV) 200,000. The fact that the unions are relatively small has encouraged centralization; without strong support from the centre many of the local units would not survive.

Board of Mediators

The Foundation of Labour has no legal power; it is purely a voluntary body. Legal responsibility for making and enforcing wage policy is vested in a Board of Mediators appointed by the Minister of Social Affairs. The functions of the Board have been to establish the general principles governing wage changes; to validate collective agreements; to declare agreements binding and to determine their scope; to fix general wage levels, establish differentials and lay down other conditions of employment.

The Board of Mediators is, from the constitutional point of view, in a curiously indeterminate position. It is expected to make its decisions within the context of Government policy, and its work falls under the aegis of the Minister of Social Affairs, who is in turn responsible to Parliament for the Board's conduct. The Minister may

[1] Mainly Socialist.

issue directions to the Board, and this is done on such questions as a change in the general level of wages, or in cases of other changes that are likely to have an important effect on the economy as a whole. The Board, however, is not simply a creature of the Government, though it has tended to give the impression, on occasion, that its principal function is to carry out official policy. The relations between the Board and the various sources of Government policy are, in fact, a matter too subtle to be expressed by a diagram of the administrative structure, or by the enunciation of a set of precise rules.[1]

It was recognized from the outset of the Netherlands' system of wage regulation that, to be successful, it needed to win the support of the unions and employers. Any attempt simply to ride roughshod over the interests of the two main parties to the contract of employment would end in failure. A statutory duty was, therefore, laid upon the Board of Mediators to consult the Foundation of Labour before any decisions of general importance to employers and workers were taken. Thus the freedom of the Board to act simply as an agent of the State authorities was limited by this duty. As events have turned out the Foundation of Labour has emerged as the gear-box in the mechanism. Demands for wage changes generated by the process of economic activity are only transmitted by the Board after they have passed through the Foundation. The Government does not wait until an issue reaches the Board before it makes its views known; official opinion is, therefore, one of the factors that the Foundation must take into account when arriving at its recommendations. Thus, in practice, the Board has tended to become a ratifying body rather than the power-centre of the system.

In 1950, the Netherlands Government decided to establish a Social and Economic Council that could advise it on the wider problems of social and economic policy. The Council is composed of persons nominated by the trade unions, employers' organizations and the Government. The establishment of this body, which is now the principal adviser to the Government on the broad issues of wages policy as well as on other economic and social questions, has had some influence on the functions and powers of both the Board and the Foundation of Labour. Since the jurisdiction of the Social and Economic Council overlapped that of the other bodies, difficulties inevitably arose, but a *modus vivendi* was arrived at albeit a somewhat uncomfortable one.[2]

---

[1] See M. G. Levenbach, 'Collective Bargaining in the Netherlands', *Modern Law Review*, October 1953.

[2] For an account of the relations between these bodies and the way in which they have discharged their functions see M. G. Levenbach, *op. cit.*

First Principles

The primary objectives which it was hoped would be achieved by the adoption of a national wage policy in the Netherlands were (1) the maintenance of economic stability by controlling the general level of wages, and (2) the establishment of equitable and satisfactory wage differentials between different occupations. It was agreed by all parties to the policy that, in principle, wages should be determined in the light of prevailing economic circumstances and estimated future developments. This end was to be secured through the institutional arrangements described, instead of by the pulls and shoves of employers and unions in an oligopolistic labour market. It was also believed that the 'crude' forces of supply and demand could be replaced as the determinants of wage relationships by a 'rational' calculation based on a sophisticated analysis of occupational differences. How far success in the attainment of these objectives has been achieved will now be examined.

The first step that was taken, when the national wage policy was introduced, was the establishment of a national minimum wage for unskilled adult workers at a level that would enable a man to maintain a family of four at a reasonable subsistence standard in the prevailing economic circumstances. Semi-skilled workers' wages were fixed at ten per cent, and skilled workers' wages at twenty per cent above the level set for the unskilled workers. Thereafter, until 1950, these wage levels were raised by a percentage figure that was approximately equal to the rise in the cost of living. Thus, real wages were deliberately kept more or less stationary in the immediate post-war years, in order to facilitate reconstruction, though a substantial improvement in the standard of living occurred simply because shortages and restrictions on consumption gradually disappeared and rationing was abolished.

Wage Policy and the Korean Crisis

The restoration of the Netherlands economy was threatened with a serious check when the Korean conflict began, since the change in the terms of trade brought about by the tense international situation led to a considerable deterioration in the balance of payments.[1] In addition the rearmament programme that was made necessary by the international situation substantially increased the burden of expenditure on defence. Since the economic stability of the country appeared to be in danger the Government, with the agreement of the unions and the employers, decided to reduce real wages. This was accom-

[1] Changes in the terms of trade tend to affect Holland to an even greater extent than the United Kingdom, since imports, measured in relation to gross national product, are twice as high.

plished by allowing prices to rise in 1951 by ten per cent, but only permitting wages to rise by five per cent. Part of the increase in prices was deliberately brought about by a drastic cut in subsidies and the imposition of taxes on luxury goods and motor vehicles.

These measures were not, however, regarded as adequate to protect the economy from inflation and a substantial reduction in investment was also decided upon. This was tackled by the issue of regulations calculated to reduce gross profit margins. The profits tax was raised and a drive was launched to collect the substantial arrears of taxation owed by private companies. The bank rate was raised by one per cent; a system of quantitative credit controls was introduced, and the capital market was further squeezed by a series of Government loans. In addition to these financial measures, expenditure on house building was reduced by restrictions on the issue of building licences. The Government then consolidated its policy by cutting down the volume of money created on its behalf.

The effect of these determined actions was to check temporarily the growth in economic activity, but the inflation was halted, and in twelve months, an adverse balance on current account with the rest of the world was turned into a very healthy surplus. Prices, which had risen, in 1951, by ten per cent over the previous year, were stabilized, but unemployment, which had been 2.0 per cent in 1950, rose to 3.5 in 1952. In spite of the increase in unemployment and a check to production in 1952, a considerable expansion in output was secured in the following year; the gross national product was fourteen per cent greater, at constant prices, in 1953 than it had been in 1950. Wages, however, were successfully limited by the policies followed by the Government, to an increase which in 1953 only restored purchasing power to the level of 1950.

It was apparent to everybody by 1953 that the crisis was over, though the Government was reluctant to relax its stringent policy too quickly lest it should undo the good that had been done. However, it was led by anxiety about the level of unemployment to take steps to encourage more investment, but at the same time it continued to resist large scale wage advances. Trade union pressure for a substantial wage increase mounted, but it was not until January 1954 that the Government finally agreed to a general rise of five per cent, and in addition permitted an extra increase of two per cent to skilled workers. The improvement in wages was welcomed by the unions, but it by no means satisfied them; they felt that workpeople were entitled to a greater share of the rising tide of prosperity and soon pressed for a further advance. In October 1954 permission was given by the Board of Mediators for another general wage increase of six per cent. This advance in wages was extremely significant, since for the first time it was not based on a rise in the cost of living, but was deliberately intended as an increase in real wages.

Conflict over Principles and Policy

The conflict over wage policy in 1954 stimulated opposition to the system, and it was suggested that central control of wages ought now to be relaxed. The unease which had developed was evident in the recommendation of the Foundation of Labour that the powers of the Board of Mediators should be transferred to a standing committee of the Social and Economic Council. Behind this proposal there lay a dispute over the basic principles upon which, up to that stage, wages policy had been determined. Though it was generally accepted in the Netherlands that the control of wage movements by the Government had helped considerably in the immediate post-war years, criticism from the employers and a section of the unions had begun to grow from the end of 1952.[1] Had it not been for the economic crisis engendered by the Korean War boom, pressure for relaxation might have come earlier.

It was, perhaps, not unnatural that as memories of the war receded, and Holland emerged from the period of reconstruction, the unity of opinion upon which the national wages policy was founded should have gradually given way to a hankering for more freedom on the part of the employers. They began to feel that their right to fix wages without the permission of the Government should be restored, if not entirely, at least to a much greater extent than had been the case since 1945. Dissatisfaction was also voiced by the Christian trade unions, and even in the socialist orientated unions, which remained in support of economic planning and the maintenance of a Government controlled wage policy, the feeling grew that changes in the system ought to be made.

The Government was not at first in favour of the suggestion that the powers of the Board of Mediators should be transferred to the Social and Economic Council; when, however, after an acute conflict, a majority of the Social and Economic Council recommended the adoption of the proposal, the Government announced that it was 'prepared in principle to move in the direction of transferring powers in the field of wage policy to organized trade and industry as represented in the Social and Economic Council'.[2] The Minister of Social Affairs also stated at the same time that the Government would

[1] See National Wage Policy: The Experience of the Netherlands. B. Zoeteweij, *International Labour Review*, Vol. LXX, No. 2, February 1955.

[2] *Amsterdamsche Bank Quarterly Review*, No. 111, Fourth Quarter 1955

instruct the Board of Mediators to consider other fundamental changes in the principles upon which wages had hitherto been determined.

A crisis was again reached when, after the two very prosperous years of 1954 and 1955, in which every segment of the economy expanded rapidly, the Government, fearing that an inflationary situation was developing, sought to check wages from rising further. The unions were not prepared to accept the Government's diagnosis and treatment of the situation; they claimed that the share of wages in the national income had fallen and that on this score they were entitled to a further rise. Faced by this demand the Government requested the Social and Economic Council to hold an inquiry into the validity of the argument; it also asked the Council to take into account the fact that controlled house-rents would be allowed to rise in 1957 and that in the same year workers would be called upon to pay old-age pension insurance premiums. The Report of the Council confirmed that officially determined wage rates had lagged to some extent, but that earnings *per capita* had risen by the same amount as the national income *per capita*.[1] On the basis of the Report it was finally agreed, after prolonged negotiations, which almost ended in the collapse of the Foundation of Labour and of the whole system of wage controls, that a maximum lump sum payment of three per cent of the annual wage should be made for the year 1955, and that in addition each industry should be allowed to raise its wages up to a maximum of six per cent. When the Government approved these recommendations in March 1956, it did so on condition that the lump sum payment was not passed on to prices and also that price increases in respect of the permitted six per cent further rise would only be allowed if the increase, in fact, did not exceed three per cent.

It turned out that, in 1956, industrial wage rates rose by a little more than three per cent over the average of 1955, but by January 1957, as a result of increases allowed, industrial wage rates had risen by eleven per cent over the level of the previous January.[2] To the increase in wages granted in 1956 should also be added the non-recurring payment of three per cent, and the additions to holiday payments and other extra-earnings allowed which, when added together, brought the total increase in labour costs in 1956 to over ten per cent, which was about six per cent more than the rise in production for the year. It was expected that much of the increase in wages would be at the expense of profits, and there is evidence that to

[1] There was an unresolved dispute as to the validity of the conclusions which arose over the correctness of the base date used.

[2] *Maandschrift*, February 1957.

some extent this has occurred. Prices were, on the average, a little less than three per cent above the average of the previous year, but there was a rapid rise in 1957 as the rise in effective demand exerted its pressures.

With all the signs in the summer of 1956 pointing to another bout of inflation, the Netherlands Government, unable to control the economic situation by means of its system of wage regulations, again took steps to curtail the demand for money. Interest rates were raised, and in June 1956 restrictions were placed on hire purchase buying. By the autumn it was apparent to the Government that a more resolute effort would have to be made if the rising spiral of prices and wages was to be curbed.

In September, the Government decided to ask the Social and Economic Council to report on how far it was necessary to reduce outlay to restore a favourable balance of payments. The Report, when published, suggested that total disbursements for the year should be cut back by two per cent. In order to achieve this result the Government eventually proposed to reduce its expenditure on consumption by Fl.50.5 million, on investment by Fl.67 million, and on war damage by Fl.10 million. The expenditure by local authorities would be trimmed by Fl.100, of which Fl.75 million would be a capital cut. In addition taxation would be increased by raising the rates of excise duty on tobacco and the turnover tax, by suspending capital expenditure allowances, and by raising the corporation tax. Subsidies on milk and sugar would be reduced and the charges made by public utilities raised.

The outstanding feature of this report was that it was a unanimous one, agreed to by representatives of both employers and trade unions

TABLE 13

	Industrial Wage Rates Adult Males	Industrial Earnings Adult Males	Prices	Unem- ployment	National Income at Constant Prices
1947	100	100	100	1.2	100
1948	105	105	103	1.1	111
1949	109	109	109	1.5	119
1950	116	117	118	2.0	123
1951	125	126	130	2.3	120
1952	128	131	132	3.5	125
1953	130	133	132	2.8	136
1954	144	148	137	1.9	145
1955	151	159	138	1.3	157
1956	156	170	142	0.9	161
1957	173	–	158	1.3	–

Sources: *Maandschrift*
Statistiek der lonen

and the independent experts. It was suggested in some quarters that it was a mistake to reduce capital expenditure, since that would impair productive capacity. This view was rejected by the Council on the grounds that it was over-simplified and failed to grasp the nature of the problem. If there had been idle factors of production waiting to be put to use, then a cut in investment expenditure would have merely intensified the problem, but this was not the case. Full employment existed and the rate at which capital expenditure was rising was generating an inflationary rise in incomes. It was, however, recognized that some forms of capital expenditure were more inflationary than others and it was proposed to reduce that type which was likely to generate a greater demand for labour. Capital projects of a labour saving variety were, as far as possible, not to be cut, since they would allow for an increase in output without putting additional pressure on the labour supply.

Following discussions in the Social and Economic Council between the employers, the unions and the Government, it was decided in December that a wage stabilization programme should be introduced in January 1957. Under this agreement the trade unions undertook not to seek further wage increases to compensate for the abolition of certain subsidies and further increases in taxation. However, wages rose by six per cent in January 1957, since it had been previously agreed that there should be an increase in wages to compensate for the rise in the contributions for old age insurance which came into effect that month. It was announced in May 1957, that agreement had been reached that wages could be allowed to rise by two per cent in August to compensate for the increase by twenty-five per cent, of statutorily controlled rents, which was permitted from July.

In their turn the employers agreed to accept the principle that no prices would be raised without first securing the approval of the Government. Maximum prices were fixed for a number of household items and later ceilings were set to the price of gas, electricity and water. The retail price index in fact rose from 115 in April to 121 in July. This increase was mainly due to a sharp rise in food prices that followed the cut in subsidies and to various seasonal and other factors.

In spite of the efforts to curtail expenditure it was apparent that the cash budget deficit would be much larger than was originally anticipated. However, it was expected that it would be possible to finance this short-fall to a large extent from savings, thus reducing the inflationary effect to a considerable extent. To strengthen the disinflationary policy embarked upon by the Government, the Netherlands Central Bank raised its discount rate to 5 per cent.

Wage Policy and Wage Structure

The award of March 1956 was not only a significant defeat for those who wished to use wage controls as the main instrument of stability, but it also modified one of the cardinal principles of the national wage policy as previously carried out. Hitherto wage differentials had been based on a national system of job evaluation and no allowance was made for the ability of one industry to pay a higher wage than another on purely market considerations. In the Report mentioned above, the Social and Economic Council recommended that in future it should be possible for enterprises to diverge from compulsory wage regulations; and the six per cent award gave effect to this recognition of the need for greater flexibility as between industries, since it was not mandatory, but permissive.

That the Netherlands authorities should have been compelled to make these concessions to factors they had sought to exclude from consideration in wage determination was an extremely significant event, since it clearly showed the limitations of the basic assumptions on which the founders of the national wages policy had based their rejection of free collective bargaining. The abstract conception of social justice which had been at the heart of the attempt to co-ordinate wages scientifically had evidently not provided either workers or employers with the satisfaction anticipated.

The founders of the Netherlands wage system held the opinion that it was socially and economically undesirable that wage standards should be based upon such differences as might occur in the profitability of enterprise, the supply and demand for labour, the bargaining strength of unions and employers and historical accident and tradition. It was felt that a stable system of wages could only be established on a basis of equity as determined by a scientific calculation of the content of each job, the conditions under which it was performed and circumstances of the performer. Thus the basic principle upon which the Netherlands wages policy rested was the notion that work should be rewarded according to social rather than economic criteria.

When the national wage policy was first introduced it was based upon three main categories of work; skilled, semi-skilled and unskilled, with a ten per cent margin between each. It was soon realized that these distinctions were too crude and would require further qualification if a satisfactory wage structure was to be developed. In some instances these main groups were broken down into four or more sub-groups. The refinements in the structure of wages were carried further by the development of a comprehensive system of work classification and job evaluation. In order to provide a sound basis for this ambitious scheme for co-ordinating wage differentials over all industry throughout the country, a committee of experts (Commission for Normalization) was set up to develop a comprehensive scheme of job evaluation and work classification. The method adopted involved the grading of jobs throughout industry according to a series of factors such as knowledge required, dexterity, care, responsibility, physical effort, risk of accident, etc. Points were then assigned according to the extent to which the factor applied to each job. The next step was to grade each job within a series of broader classifications and to convert the points rating into wages. An allowance was made for differences in the cost of living and the country was divided into five wage zones. Each employer had to comply with the basic wage rates as laid down in the regulations, but the detailed application of the standard scheme of job evaluation to particular industries was not made compulsory; its complete adoption was left to the voluntary decision of the employers and unions concerned.[1]

Since the wages policy involved not only the control of minimum but also of maximum wages, any change in wage structure had to be notified by the Board of Mediators. Evasion would have been a simple matter had the regulations been confined to basic wage rates; control had, therefore, to be extended to cover every kind of allowance, bonus or payment for overtime and shift-work, holiday pay, pensions and welfare scheme. Piece rates were permitted so long as they did not exceed rather narrow limits and special arrangements were made for time workers to benefit by an approved system of merit rating. Thus, every aspect of wage determination in Holland has been made subject to regulation and settled in accordance with national policy.

TABLE 14

Index of average weekly earnings of adult male workers in industry

	Skilled	Semi-skilled	Unskilled
1939	100	100	100
1947	186	199	213
1947	100	100	100
1955	161	160	161
	Per cent	*Per cent*	*Per cent*
1939	100	86	77
1947	100	92	87
1955	100	91	88

Source: *Statistiek der lonen*

[1] There are about 200 separate industrial groups for which regulations have been made. In addition the Board has to deal with separate wage schemes for individual enterprises not belonging to an industry covered by a general regulation, and for numerous individual enterprises with exceptions from the general rules of their industry; altogether about 6,000 cases per annum. Levenbach, *op. cit.*

It will be seen from these figures that there has been little or no change in the earning differentials since 1947. The actual differential, it will be noticed, is rather less than the twenty per cent planned. The general pattern which these figures reveal does not differ markedly from that which has emerged in other countries. The narrowing process, by comparison with Britain, seems to have gone slightly further in the Netherlands.[1] This is not, however, entirely the consequence of the national wage policy, since the trend was well established long before its introduction. It is possible that the trend would have gone further had a national wage policy not been pursued, but since there has been pressure in favour of wider differentials it may well be that the centralization of wage determination has prevented a shift towards wider differentials.

Average hourly earnings of women workers as a proportion of male workers' earnings fell from sixty-two per cent in 1947 to sixty per cent in 1955.[2] This slight change was in the opposite direction from that taken in the United Kingdom, in which the average hourly earnings of women workers in manufacturing industry rose from fifty-eight per cent in 1947 to sixty per cent in 1955.[3] It is difficult to believe that the fall in the proportion of women's earnings was deliberately contrived in the Netherlands, since this would hardly have been in harmony with the general principles of greater equality on which the national wage policy is based. The fall was probably due to factors in the labour market that could not be offset.

Whatever effect the national wage policy might have had on wage relationships, the interference with the freedom of employers and workers mutually to make readjustments has steadily grown more onerous. One of the principal architects of the Netherlands wage policy has admitted that 'a system of wage control by a central board is more rigid than a system of free wages. Moreover it is of necessity more long-winded and clumsy. Also the Board at the top tends to be far away, impersonal and a more or less nebulous entity'.[4] These are big disadvantages to overcome, and it is not surprising that this authority should write 'everybody constantly expresses a hope for more freedom and for the lessening of controls'.

It would be wrong to conclude that the efforts made under the aegis of the Foundation of Labour by employers and unions to reshape the structure of wages in the Netherlands had been fruitless. The wide application of the standard method of job evaluation

[1] For British figures see Reynolds and Taft, *op. cit.*
[2] *Statistiek der lonen*, October–December 1955.
[3] *Ministry of Labour Gazette*, September 1956.
[4] Levenbach, *op. cit.*

I

developed by a committee of experts (the Netherlands Commission for Normalization) has almost certainly resulted in better intra-firm wage structures. In addition it has also probably contributed a great deal to the considerable rise in productivity achieved in the Netherlands during the past few years. Whenever a systematic job analysis is done it always brings to light inefficiencies that were not obvious, even though suspected. On the basis of the information obtained it is often possible to secure agreement to changes that would, in other circumstances, be resisted. Thus the intensive use of work study for the purpose of achieving an equitable wage structure has been of great benefit to industry in the Netherlands, in spite of the fact that the primary objective of achieving greater equity, as determined by planning rather than by bargaining, has proved to have serious disadvantages.

Wage Policy and Inflation: An Evaluation

There is no escaping from the simple fact that its elaborate system of wage controls has not saved Holland from an inflation like that suffered by most other countries. The movement of wages and prices over the post-war period has been remarkably similar to that which has occurred elsewhere. It is, indeed, the similarities in the Dutch economic scene, rather than the differences, which impress the onlooker.

Wage rates may well have been kept down below the market equilibrium level. There is good reason for believing that this has been the case, since earnings, as in other countries, have tended to pull away from the established wage rates. There is also evidence that a certain degree of evasion of the maximum limits set to wages by the regulations has taken place. It is impossible to put a figure to the extent to which 'black' wages are paid, but it is admitted by both employers and trade unionists that this development has been a cause of stress and strain.

The limitation on wage increases was undoubtedly an important feature of the emergency programme, launched in 1951, to save the balance of payments from further deterioration. But it is abundantly clear that wage controls alone would not have succeeded in completely altering the whole economic outlook in the manner achieved. It was the conjunction of vigorously applied counter-inflationary economic policies, coupled with the restraint of the unions, which permitted the astonishing recovery.

One of the major difficulties of tackling inflation by means of wage controls is that the prevention of wage increases builds up a tremendous pressure which, when released, results in an explosion. This is precisely what happened in Holland in 1950–51, 1953–54 and again in 1956. Strict wage restraint can, therefore, never be more than a temporary state of affairs in an economic situation in which there is a strong demand pull. On each occasion when wages rose rapidly in the Netherlands a restocking and investment boom was under way. It was the rising demand for resources, stimulated by an active budgetary and monetary policy that created the conditions under which the supply price of labour could be easily pushed up by the unions. When it was absolutely necessary to check the expansion, because of the deterioration in the balance of payments, investment was curbed and stocks were drawn down. If this had not been brought about, there would have been no fall in the demand for labour and wage regulation would not have been effective. This is surely proved by the way in which the regulation and restraint collapsed when stocks had to be rebuilt and new investment expended.

The essential lesson to be learnt from the experience of the Netherlands is not that inflation can be prevented by wage controls. Inflation can, of course, be prevented by wage controls as long as they are carried out with totalitarian ruthlessness. But in a democratic society it is impossible to insulate the instruments of wage determination from the pressures generated by the inter-play of economic forces. In these circumstances, stability can only be achieved by resolute and persistent control of the factors which lead so easily to an over-rapid expansion of effective demand. The inflation was checked in the Netherlands when the Government, with the support of the unions and of the employers, pressed its disinflationary economic policies to the point of creating a serious rise in unemployment. It is at this point that wage restraint becomes highly significant, since if the unions are willing to hold back their demands and employers, in the change from a soft to a hard market environment, cease to bid up the price of labour, costs may fall faster than revenue. Inflation may, therefore, be checked quickly and without the necessity of draconic budgetary and monetary measures. But if the check is to be converted into a stable trend permanent reliance cannot be placed on wage controls; it must be placed on fiscal and monetary policies that will maintain a level of effective demand that does not constantly induce wages to rise above the level that would permit of price stability.

The adoption of a centralized system of wage determination is only compatible with free trade unionism and free enterprise so long as it responds to the economic and political pressures that are generated in a free society. It is, therefore, impossible to eliminate bargaining pressures by establishing a centralized system of wage determination. The experience of the Netherlands amply confirms this generalization, since bargaining was not eliminated by the establishment of the Foundation of Labour and of the Social and Economic Council; it was simply transferred from the local to the national level. It is possible to argue, as many supporters of national wage policy have done, that this is all to the good, since it means that the issues can be thrashed out against the background of the national economic situation. But whilst this may be so, it does not follow that the results will be an improvement on those that would have been reached by decentralized, sectional bargaining. It has been demonstrated that unions will temporarily accept a policy of wage restraint which has been decided on the basis of a national agreement, but it is also possible, under a centralized system, for the unions to insist on the Government adopting, as the price of their acceptance of temporary wage restraint, policies that permit of an over-rapid expansion of income at a later stage, simply because they bank up the pressure of excess demand rather than remove it. Ultimately the outcome of any system of bargaining, whether it be a centralized one like that adopted in the Netherlands, a decentralized one like that of Britain, or an even more decentralized one like that of America will depend upon the power of the contending factions. If the unions are strong and the general economic and political circumstances are favourable, they will be in a position, whatever the formal institutional arrangements through which collective bargaining is carried on, to push wages to levels which in conjunction with investment demand make inflation inevitable. If there is excess demand and the unions do not push wages up, employers will pull the level up for themselves.

No country has made a greater effort than the Netherlands to control economic activity by planning and by the careful use of regulations. The nation is extremely well served by the supply of statistical information; on the staff of the Central Planning Bureau are to be found some of the most brilliant economists in Europe; yet these advantageous factors have not proved to be an adequate basis for achieving economic stability. Failure has been due, not to a lack of knowledge, but to the difficulty of persuading people to act in a manner which seems contrary to their immediate interests. Everybody has wanted a bigger share of the available resources, and the methods employed to keep total demand in step with supply have only succeeded at the expense of a rise in prices not very different from that which has occurred in many other countries. Like other countries that were determined to maintain full employment after the war, the Netherlands pursued a cheap money policy in the belief that the interest rate was an outmoded instrument of regulation. This point of view seems to have undergone a significant change in 1956 and 1957 since the bank rate was gradually raised to five per cent; much the highest rate since the war. It will be interesting to see whether the authorities will be able to maintain greater stability in the future, now that they have overcome their previous inhibitions against making money a dear as well as a cheap commodity.

Wage Policy and Industrial Relations
Finally it is necessary to consider the impact of the centralized system of wage controls on industrial relations. It has frequently been claimed that the participation of the unions in the determination of over-all economic policy has resulted in a vast improvement in industrial relations. Claims of this kind are necessarily extremely difficult to test, since the problem of measurement is almost insuperable. However, it is possible to examine strike statistics which provide some, though by no means complete, evidence of the state of industrial relations.

From Table 15 it will be seen that the number of disputes during the post-war years fell sharply after 1951. It is tempting to attribute this improvement in industrial relations to the system of wage determination, but it cannot be overlooked that a similar dramatic improvement occurred in the 1930's, though, of course, in quite different circumstances. If the years 1955 and 1956 are taken out of the last group then the picture becomes rather different, since the average number of working days has risen from 88.8 thousand per year for the whole of the period to 172.8 thousand per year. This might lead to the conclusion that there is a growing dissatisfaction with the system, which has only been assuaged at the expense of a significant relaxation in the amount of control exercised over wage changes.

TABLE 15

	Average number of Disputes per year		Average number of Working Days lost per year	
	Netherlands	UK	Netherlands	UK
1926–1930	220	357	446,100	32,259,000
1931–1935	184	438	644,000	3,497,000
1936–1939	105	940	81,500	1,957,000
1946–1950	184	1,690	293,700	1,946,000
1951–1956	69	1,871	88,800	2,305,000

Sources: *Jaarcijfers voor Nederland: Central Bureau voor de Statistiek*
Ministry of Labour Gazette

By comparison with Britain, the Netherlands has an enviable record of industrial peace during the past six years; but it is difficult to prove that this favourable situation is due entirely to the difference in methods of wage settlement. Since the number of working days lost per thousand employed was substantially lower in Holland before the war, it is likely that more fundamental economic and social factors were the principal causes of the trends in both countries. The record of social stability in the Netherlands, when measured by many other indicators such as divorce, suicide, crime, alcoholic and drug addict figures,[1] is one which would lead to the expectation of relatively low strike figures.

It would be foolish to deny that the system of wage determination has had any significant impact on industrial relations. Employers and unions have shown themselves willing and able to take decisions that are in the interest of the whole nation, but it must not be overlooked that the very need to take such decisions as to accept a temporary reduction in real incomes has only arisen because previous demands, which exceeded the country's capacity, were satisfied. Both sides of industry have shown, in fact, that they are primarily motivated by their own interests and that they are not willing to sacrifice their sectional interests beyond a point that generally stops short of maintaining economic stability, unless compelled by factors beyond their immediate control.

[1] Cf. *The Economist*, August 17, 1957

CHAPTER 9

Wages and Economic
Stability in Germany

The Germans have long been famed as a hardworking, disciplined people who are capable of astonishing effort when they dedicate themselves to a task. True to their tradition, and by an immense feat of labour, in a decade they have raised the truncated western half of Germany that had been left a stricken ruin by the war to a proud and prosperous nation.

The economic recovery of the German Republic is one of the most remarkable achievements in modern European economic history. Since the currency reform of 1948 industrial production has increased at a rate far surpassing that of any other country in Europe. Germany's exports have expanded at such a pace that they have almost become an embarrassment. Taxes have been reduced, social services have been considerably improved, and wages, salaries and profits have risen substantially. Prices withal have been held to a much lower rate of increase than in any of the other countries which have been examined here. What, might well be asked is, the secret of this phenomenal tale of success?

The recovery of Germany has been achieved with the minimum of physical controls. It may, in fact, be said to have dated from the currency reform, which was accompanied by the sweeping away of rationing and price controls and by substantial tax reductions. These drastic measures restored incentives and offered handsome rewards to private enterprise. The immediate result was the end of the black market, a rapid increase in output and the commencement of a rise in real income. Some non-German economists, reared in the Keynesian tradition, thought that this policy was doomed to failure; having pinned their faith in physical controls and decided that an economy could not be safely guided by monetary measures, they could not believe that the policies followed by the Germans could work and, moreover, work exceptionally well.

The success of the monetary policy of the Bank Deutscher Länder (the Central Bank) and the fiscal policy of the Federal Government may be measured by the rate of investment, which from 1949 has been about the highest in Europe, and by the stability of the purchasing power of the D-Mark, which compares extremely favourably with the value of the currency of any of the major industrial countries.

Monetary Policy

The Bank Deutscher Länder has taken the view from the beginning of the recovery that it must prevent the value of the D-Mark from being depreciated by inflation. The financial system of Western Germany is very different in many respects from that of Britain, but the policy pursued by the Bank Deutscher Länder has been to control borrowing by means of the rate of interest, and to control the supply of money by the direct regulation of the reserve requirements of the commercial banks and of their short-term lending.

During the Korean War the discount rate was raised to six per cent and various other measures were taken to prevent the supply of money rising too rapidly. The cost of living rose, but not by as much as in many other countries. The holding down of the German price level to a rise of twelve per cent from 1950 to 1956 may be compared with a price rise in Britain during this period of forty per cent.

TABLE 16
Hourly Wages in Manufacturing Industry[1]

	Holland		Sweden		UK		USA		Germany	
	wages	prices	wages	prices	wages	prices	wages	prices	wages	prices
1948	80	–	63	77	74	77	76	90	–	–
1949	81	81	65	78	77	79	79	90	–	–
1950	89	88	68	79	80	81	82	90	78	93
1951	95	99	84	91	87	89	90	97	89	100
1952	98	100	98	98	95	97	94	99	96	102
1953	100	100	100	100	100	100	100	100	100	100
1954	111	104	104	101	106	102	102	100	103	100
1955	120	106	111	104	114	106	106	100	109	102
1956	128	109	120	109	123	112	112	102	119	105

When this achievement is considered it is necessary to take into account that at the same time a much higher rate of investment was being financed and wages were rising almost as fast as in Britain. Why, then, did not the Germans experience a degree of inflation similar to that which occurred in Britain? There seem to be three main reasons why the Germans have been more fortunate in keeping their economy under better control: (1) a rapidly increasing labour supply, (2) an enormous increase in productivity, (3) trade union policy.

Labour Supply

The total number of employees rose from 13.9 million in 1950 to 18.1 million in 1956. This exceptionally rapid increase in the labour force

[1] OEEC Bulletin of General Statistics.

was, as is well known, due mainly to the great influx of refugees from
the Soviet-controlled East Germany. The refugees were at first looked
upon as an economic burden, but they have, in fact, proved to be a
tremendous windfall, enabling an investment boom to continue at an
extraordinary pace without producing an inflation. Instead of the
rising demand for labour leading to wage increases which exceeded
the rise in output, the pressure in the labour market was reduced by
the continuous increase in the supply of workers.

TABLE 17

	Employment	Unemployment
1950	100	10.0
1951	105	9.0
1952	107	8.4
1953	113	7.5
1954	118	7.0
1955	124	5.1
1956	130	4.2

The increase in the supply of workers was aided by the length of
the working week, which rose from 48 hours to 48.8 in 1955 and has
since fallen back to 48. Since earnings above the normal rates of pay
received for Sunday, holiday, night shift and overtime are exempt
from income tax payments in Germany, workers have been encouraged to work the number of hours employers have desired. The
fall in the hours worked since 1955 has been due to a reduction in the
basic working week; but if the level of demand for labour continues to
rise, it is expected to have the effect of raising wage costs, as more
work will have to be paid for at the higher rates. Much depends on
the future supply of labour; sooner or later the flow of refugees will
dry up and demand may then rapidly overtake supply. The ability of
the authorities to maintain full employment with as small a rise in
prices as experienced since 1950 will then be more effectively tested.

Investment and Productivity
The ample supplies of labour permitted full use to be made of an
exceptionally high rate of capital investment. Gross domestic fixed
capital investment rose to 26.4 per cent of the gross national product
in 1955. This great expansion in investment activity was financed
primarily by private savings and the ploughing back of industrial
profits.

These savings were a vital factor in the prevention of inflation; had
they not been forthcoming the expansion of bank lending would
almost certainly have led to an inflationary rise in prices. Special
measures were introduced to encourage private savings instead of
consumption. It was possible, if certain conditions were fulfilled, to

deduct savings from income as a tax relief. It has been calculated that this concession could mean that in the first year an effective rate of interest of fifty per cent might be earned on savings.[1]

Industrial savings on a large scale were made possible by the high level of profits that were earned. These were, in turn, the result of moderate wage policies. But tax provisions that favoured investment, such as depreciation allowances, and others which discouraged high dividends, were a powerful incentive to expand investment.

The supply of savings from private sources was further augmented by public savings. In this connection the achievement of a considerable Budget surplus from 1952 helped a great deal. The Federal German Republic would have had a far more difficult problem of public finance to face had it been compelled to spend as much on defence as the United Kingdom. Since social security provisions for old age, invalidity, survivors, sickness, maternity, industrial injury, unemployment, family allowances and health services, are financed in Germany, to a far greater extent than is the case in Britain, by a charge on employers and employees, there has been on that score less strain on public revenues.

TABLE 18

Percentage Distribution of Sources of Revenue of Five Major Social Security Schemes, 1955[2]

	Government	Insured Persons	Employers	Others
Germany	15.9	30.3	51.2	2.6
UK	47.8	19.8	26.6	5.9

American aid was an important source of capital in the early years of the German recovery, but in later years the huge surplus earned on the foreign trade account has been of great significance as the fount of new capital for German industry.

The flow of funds provided the essential capital, but a prodigious effort on the part of workers and managers was required to take full advantage of the resources made available. How well the Germans succeeded is eloquently expressed by Table 19.

From the point of view of maintaining stable prices the rise in output per man was more important than the general rise in production. Although the increase was not as spectacular as total production it was very rapid. But, even more significantly, wage costs per unit of output rose by very much less than in most other European countries.

[1] F. Lutz, 'Germany's Economic Resurgence', *Lloyds Bank Review*, January 1956.
[2] Wages and Related Elements of Labour Cost in European Industry, 1955, ILO Geneva 1957.

TABLE 19[1]

| | Industrial Production | | | Gross National Product | |
	Germany	UK		Germany	UK
1950	100	100		100	100
1951	117	104		120	103
1952	126	101		139	106
1953	139	107		148	105
1954	156	115		157	109
1955	179	126		172	114
1956	193	120		190	117

TABLE 20
Manufacturing Industry

| | Productivity per Man-Hour | | Hourly Earnings | | Wage Costs per unit of Output | |
	Germany	UK	Germany	UK	Germany	UK
1950	100	100	100	100	100	100
1951	108	101	115	109	107	108
1952	112	99	123	118	110	120
1953	119	102	129	125	108	122
1954	125	108	132	133	106	124
1955	133	111	141	143	106	129
1956	138	110	153	153	111	139

Source: H. H. Liesner, 'Relative Costs and Prices in British, American and German Manufacturing Industry', *London and Cambridge Economic Bulletin*, September 1956, *Monthly Digest of Statistics*, *Ministry of Labour Gazette*.

The comparison of wage costs per unit of output is particularly striking in the case of Britain and Germany. In making a comparison of labour costs between different countries it is necessary to bear in mind that other factors apart from wages enter into a full assessment. For example, such items as holidays with pay, social insurance premiums, expenditures on canteens, welfare facilities and other amenities must be taken into account since they form a very large proportion of total labour costs in some countries. In the case of Germany it has recently been estimated by the ILO that defined non-wage elements in a selected number of manufacturing industries amounted to twenty-six per cent of total labour cost. The United Kingdom figure on the same basis was eleven per cent. When, however, total labour costs per hour were compared the average hourly earnings of British workers were much higher, as Table 21 shows. These comparisons are subject to a margin of error, but the figures seem reasonably consistent, though it should be borne in mind that wage costs per hour are not the same as wage costs per unit of product, nor do they measure differences in income standards. It is apparent, however, that as a result of changes in productivity and wages, labour

[1] Derived from OEEC *Bulletin of General Statistics*,

costs have risen to a far smaller extent in Germany than in Britain since 1950.

TABLE 21
Wages and Selected Elements in Labour Costs in Swiss Francs

	Germany	UK	Ratio
Cotton Textiles			
Average hourly earnings	1.47	2.00	136
Total cost per hour	1.86	2.27	122
Leather Footwear			
Average hourly earnings	1.47	2.11	144
Total cost per hour	1.86	2.37	126
Machine Tools			
Average hourly earnings	1.83	2.78	152
Total cost per hour	2.43	3.08	126
Shipbuilding			
Average hourly earnings	1.93	2.99	155
Total cost per hour	2.49	3.27	130
Steel Industry			
Average hourly earnings	2.58	2.97	115
Total cost per hour	3.56	3.29	93
Coal Mining			
Average hourly earnings	2.35	3.56	151
Total cost per hour	3.82	4.26	111

Source: *Wages and Related Elements of Labour Cost in European Industry, 1955, Preliminary Report,* ILO, Geneva 1957.

Wages

The German trade unions have in some quarters been praised for their moderate and responsible wages policy. In others they have been criticized for not pressing their claims with greater vigour. The German unions have undoubtedly behaved with circumspection, but this may be due as much to a realistic appraisal of their strength as to a deliberate policy of restraint. The unions in Germany are almost certainly not as strong as their size and propaganda would suggest.

There are several reasons for the relative weakness of the German trade unions. One important factor is the considerable strength of the organized employers. German industry has been traditionally cartel-minded and industrialists are strongly inclined to act together in the face of trade union demands. Since the unions are organized on a geographical and industry-wide basis, collective bargaining takes place between large units of organization. At first sight this position does not seem to differ greatly from that which exists in Great Britain, but there is, in fact, a very substantial difference.

The German unions are extremely weak at the plant level. 'The unions are not equipped to utilize the "whipsaw" tactic of playing one employer against another in contract negotiations or grievance settlements. They have no plant organizations which can push for and obtain separate and more favourable contracts from individual employers. Nor do they have much to do with grievances. These are initially processed by the unaffiliated works councils (shop steward committees locally elected in each plant) and may subsequently be referred to governmental Labour Courts which follow fairly uniform settlement lines. Beyond lack of the weapon, the unions favour uniformity of treatment not only of organized but unorganized employees as well.'[1]

The weakness of the German trade union at the plant level would suggest that the problem of the wage drift is much less likely to occur there than in Britain. The actual movement of wage rates and earnings does appear to bear out this conclusion. Wage rates had increased over 1949 by 62.8 per cent in 1956 and earnings had gone up during the same period by 67.6. In the rather longer period from April 1947 to October 1956, wage rates in Britain rose by 66 per cent and earnings by 94 per cent. The main reason for the closer relation between wage rates and earnings in Germany may, however, be less the differences in institutional organization and behaviour than to the lower pressures which have been experienced in the labour market. Some support for this point of view may be derived from the tendency for earnings to draw away from wage rates after 1953 as the demand for labour expanded and the basic working week was reduced. Notwithstanding the high degree of discipline among German employers, if the demand for labour continues to rise and unemployment falls below three per cent, it will be surprising if a wage drift does not become a feature of the German economy as has occurred in the other high employment countries.

TABLE 22[a]
Annual Percentage increase in Industrial

	Wage Rates	Earnings
1950	7.7	8.0
1951	13.8	15.1
1952	7.8	7.9
1953	4.6	4.4
1954	2.5	2.9
1955	6.3	6.9
1956	8.7	9.5
1957	9.1	

There is no sign that the German unions are prepared to accept some kind of overriding national wage policy. A pamphlet recently published by the German trade unions repudiates the notion of

[1] C. Kerr, 'Collective Bargaining in Germany', *Contemporary Collective Bargaining*, Ed. A. Sturmthal (1957).

[a] *Wirtschaftswissenschaftliches Institut der Gewerkschaften.*

basing wage increases on any calculation of productivity. It is suggested that wages cannot be determined in isolation, since they are a dynamic factor in the economic system. The constant pressure for higher wages leads to the more efficient use of resources and higher output, it is argued; but in stressing the importance of the dynamic effects of the trade unions' efforts to push up wages the author is careful to add that the unions have not gone beyond the bounds of economic possibilities; nor will they do so in the future. The German trade unions, it is claimed, are in favour of the maximum rate of economic growth and of stabilized prices and they will take these objectives into account in the future as they have done in the past.[1]

The German trade unions clearly feel that they have acted with restraint and responsibility. They point to the fact that Germany stands alone, among western industrial countries, as the one instance where until 1956 productivity has risen faster than basic wage rates. There is reason to believe that they will increase their pressure for further wage increases even though the pace at which output had been increasing greatly slowed down in 1956 and 1957. The Federal Government has experienced alarm at the rising level of wage advances and it has countered the demands of the Metal Workers' Union in October 1957 for a ten per cent increase with threats and cajolements. The Chancellor, Dr Adenauer, speaking in the Bundestag, is reported as having gone so far as to say that labour would not be permitted to negotiate agreements that would endanger the economy.[2] The attitude of the Federal Government was probably influenced by the rebuff it had received when shortly before it had tried to persuade the Ruhr coalowners not to raise prices to offset an increase in costs. It remains to be seen whether the German Government will attempt to reintroduce compulsory arbitration, which was a feature of industrial relations under the Weimar constitution, if the trade unions exercise their full bargaining strength. This is undoubtedly a possibility with which the unions must reckon. It is unlikely, however, that they would accept such a measure without a bitter struggle. Compulsory arbitration is regarded by many authorities as one of the principal reasons why the pre-Hitler trade unions became too dependent upon the State. Since the rebirth of German trade unionism in 1947 the tradition of independence seems to have taken root. It is important that the foundations of this independence and vitility should not be undermined, since much more than a stable economy depends upon the ability of the German unions to maintain their freedom from domination by the State. The success of the post-

[1] Professor Bruno Gleitze, *Productivitat, Lohn, Arbeitszeit* (1957).
[2] *The Times*, November 1, 1957.

war economic policies have made an enormous contribution to the re-establishment of political democracy in Germany. From the point of view of the rest of Europe it is essential that economic growth and stability should be maintained without the taking of steps that would threaten the freedom and independence of voluntary organizations.

Strikes are regarded with particular abhorrence by the German authorities and it will be hard for them to learn to recognize that a fierce spasm of industrial unrest may be a price that has to be paid for the maintenance of a free economy. The strike record of the German trade unions is, so far, a very good one. In the period since 1950, the number of working days lost in Germany, per 10,000 workers employed, has been less than half the number lost in the United Kingdom.

It is possible that out of a rise in industrial tension might come a general agreement on wages policy between the Deutscher Gewerkschaftsbund (the German TUC) and the Federal Employers' Association. Suggestions have been made by the Employers' leader, which point to a willingness of the employers to enter into some kind of mutual pact or understanding. The incentive to enter into some arrangement is likely to grow as the labour market becomes increasingly tight.

The extent to which German trade unions and employers find it possible to work together, in spite of their antipathetic statements, has been demonstrated by the Mitbestimmung experiment in the coal and steel industries.

The all-out effort made by the German trade unions to obtain the so-called right of co-determination in the coal and steel industries, in 1950 and 1951, had, in the opinion of some informed observers, the effect of diverting attention from wage claims. It is perfectly possible that, in exchange for some share in the making of general policy, the unions would be prepared to accept a national agreement which would have the effect of moderating wage demands. Whether such a policy would survive the pressure of overfull employment it is impossible to say. In the case of Sweden such a policy has failed because of the wage drift induced by the willingness of employers as individuals to pay more than the agreement. It is possible that the discipline of the German employers may be proof against competition to obtain the labour they might desperately require.

If a national wage policy of this kind were to emerge in Germany in the future it would raise some important problems. Since the level of wages would be lower than the equilibrium, profits would tend to be above normal. The unions would almost certainly ask for some share in the use of the excess profits. They may ask that they should be used for developing socially desirable projects. It is unlikely that German industrialists would be prepared to give the unions a right of veto over the reinvestment of profits, but they might be prepared to set up a special fund, analogous to the Director's fund in a Soviet Russian enterprise, control over which would be vested jointly with management and the unions.

A further suggestion that has been made in Germany is that a certain proportion of the excess profits should be placed to the credit of the workers, only to be withdrawn after a certain time period, or when the economic situation would benefit. In other words, this would be a system of deferred wage payments, or put in still another way, forced savings.

The problem of maintaining a stable price level at a very high level of employment has not yet been faced in Germany. This is the essential reason explaining why prices have risen to a smaller extent than in other countries. To say this is not, however, to minimize the great productive effort of the Germans, the extremely well-directed monetary and fiscal policies, and the moderation of the unions. However, the real test is still to come, and it will be fascinating to see whether the problem can be solved within the framework of the policies which, so far, have been so successfully pursued.

CHAPTER 10

Wage Policy under the Conservatives

When the Conservative Government was returned to office in 1951, it was widely believed that it would pursue a policy which would check the inflation which had been a feature of the British economy since the end of the war. The price controls and licensing arrangements in which the Labour Party had placed such great faith, but which had been such a conspicuous failure from the point of view of maintaining economic stability, and had to some extent already been dismantled, were almost entirely swept away. Instead of physical controls the Conservatives promised to use the classic instruments of monetary and fiscal policy to achieve economic stability. In the first six years of office they were, however, no more successful in preventing inflation than were their predecessors in the previous six years. The Conservative lack of success was not due so much to the inadequacy of their chosen instruments as to unwillingness to use them adequately.

It will be seen from Table 23 that the growth in production was checked in the first year of office as the Conservatives struggled to bring the inflationary pressures under control. Wages were rising sharply, but the increase in unemployment brought a change in the labour market and the rate of advance slowed down. Labour costs, which had soared, did not immediately fall as production was cut back in 1952, but they rose only slightly in 1953 and 1954. Thereafter, however, as the pace of wage increases again gathered momentum, they moved up rapidly in concert. Yet in spite of the addition to costs the increase in productivity was reflected in higher real wages. By the end of 1956 workers were twenty-five per cent better off than they had been in 1948. Of this increase two-thirds had been achieved after 1953.

In the light of figures shown in Table 23 a foreigner might well conclude that the trade unions would be delighted with the net results of the Government's economic policy. Such a conclusion, as will be seen from a closer examination of the course of events, would be entirely erroneous. Most workers felt that they had been cheated out of two-thirds of the money gains which they had made and they

K

TABLE 25

Changes in Employment and Output and Incomes in the UK

	Unemployment	Ratio of Notified Vacancies to number of unemployed in March	Gross Domestic Product	Increase in Aggregate Wages	Increase in Aggregate Salaries	Increase in Labour Cost per unit of Output	Increase in Prices of Goods and Services Sold on the Home Market	Increase in Real Wages
	per cent							
1948	1.8	1.7	100	100	100	100	100	100
1949	1.6	1.1	105	106	108	102	103	104
1950	1.5	1.0	109	110	115	105	106	106
1951	1.2	1.5	112	122	129	112	116	108
1952	2.1	0.7	111	131	139	120	123	106
1953	1.8	0.6	116	138	146	122	126	108
1954	1.5	0.8	123	147	156	125	128	113
1955	1.2	1.3	127	161	171	132	133	119
1956	1.3	1.4	128	176	185	142	140	123
1957	1.6	0.6	130[1]	187[1]	196[1]	148[1]	145[1]	126[1]

Sources: Ministry of Labour Gazette, London and Cambridge Economic Bulletin and National Income and Expenditure

[1] Estimated

blamed the Government for this loss, rather than praising it for the remarkable increase in real incomes which they had secured. Though salaried employees would appear to have fared not badly, they had not advanced as rapidly as is suggested by the figures for the aggregate increase; since their numbers have been rising at the bottom of the scale, *per capita* figures would show that the incomes of salary earners have tended to lag behind those of wage earners. From 1948 to 1956, it is known that the average wage per operative employed in manufacturing industry rose from £280 to about £485 per year, an increase of seventy-three per cent; the average salary of administrators, technical and clerical workers rose in the same period to approximately £700, but this is an increase of only forty-eight per cent.[1] The gain of the wage earner would be even greater after tax.

The Attitude of the Unions
There was considerable speculation as to what would be the attitude of the unions under a Conservative Government. Fears were expressed that the unions might use their industrial strength to prevent the Conservatives from carrying out their economic policy. Fears of this kind were set at rest when, at its first meeting following the General Election, the General Council of the Trades Union Congress issued a declaration of its intentions. It stated: 'We shall continue to examine every question solely in the light of its industrial and economic implication. The Trade Union Movement must always be free to formulate and advocate its own policies. . . . In the future, as in the past, we shall urge on the Government those policies which, from our experience, we believe to be in the best interests of the country as a whole and from the same standpoint we shall retain our right to disagree and publicly oppose the Government where we think it is necessary to do so.'[2]

This statement did no more, in fact, than set out the fundamental principle of trade union autonomy, irrespective of party, which had been followed throughout the whole period of trade union history. Although the trade unions have always been much concerned with politics, and they have been closely associated, first with the Liberal Party and, for the past fifty years, with the Labour Party, they have never been prepared to allow purely party political considerations to govern their attitude and policy. On this question the opinion of the General Council of the TUC was unequivocally expressed in 1938, when it passed a resolution relating to the duties of the unions in relation to rearmament which stated: 'That the General Council

[1] *Bulletin for Industry.*
[2] *Labour,* November 1951.

places on record its conviction that in dealing with any Government on behalf of the trade union movement its conduct must be determined by industrial and not political considerations. Further, that in regard to the appeal of the Prime Minister on the acceleration of the Rearmament Programme we regard this as exclusively a matter for the trade union movement.'[1]

This attitude was reaffirmed when suggestions were made that the unions should call strikes to obstruct the denationalization of industry; the General Council refused to depart from the position it had consistently taken since the General Strike, that the industrial strength of the unions should not be used for the achievement of political ends.

It would, of course, be foolish not to recognize that the close links between the trade unions and the Labour Party give the Labour Party an advantage in making an appeal to the unions to act with restraint in making wage claims. Though the trade unions are not prepared to compromise their independence, sympathy with the aims of the Labour Party and loyalty to the ideals held in common, naturally exert some influence on the behaviour of the unions. This influence is, however, not so great as might be suggested by the fact that the unions provide the Labour Party with the bulk of its members and of its funds.

The General Council of the TUC was well aware of the critical economic situation which threatened the country in the winter of 1951 and summer of 1952. Under the leadership of Arthur Deakin, who had been convinced of the threat which excessive wage increases presented to the maintenance of full employment, the Council urged the unions to recognize the danger that was involved in reckless demands for higher wages. An attempt by the Communist-led Electrical Trades Union specifically to disavow 'the Tory Government's policy of so-called "restraint" or "moderation" designed to secure the withholding of such wage claims' was defeated by a majority of over two million at the 1952 Trades Union Congress. But at this same Congress the delegates gave short shrift to a proposal that the General Council should review the existing machinery for wage-fixing and negotiations and 'report whether greater co-ordination is desirable with a view to providing greater equity and fairer relativities in the rewards for labour in all branches of private and public employment'. Replying for the General Council, Sir Thomas Williamson claimed that the intention of the proposers was 'to put Congress into a preliminary canter directed towards the vague and academic proposal expounded during the past few years for a national

[1] TUC *Annual Report*, 1938, p. 298.

wages policy'. Such a notion was, he implied, clearly beneath contempt, and the Chairman, Mr Deakin, was obviously of the same mind, since he characteristically told the mover, when the latter was seeking to exercise his right of reply, 'You are entitled to reply, but that is how I regard it—as a sheer waste of time'.[1] And so it proved.

The General Council of the TUC was ready to recommend the continuance of a responsible wage policy. And it went so far as to declare that 'wage moderation is more than a political matter, to be used discriminately to help one government or another'.[2] But the Council would not agree to countenance any interference with the traditional autonomy of the wage-fixing arrangements. When, in December 1951, the Minister of Labour refused to confirm a unanimous decision of a Wages Council to tie wages in the industry concerned to a cost of living sliding scale, a protest was at once made. In the following May and June the Minister, following a precedent set by a Labour predecessor, delayed his usually automatic confirmation of decisions arrived at by Wages Councils. At the request of the Union of Shop, Distributive and Allied Workers, the General Council, as they had done on the previous occasion, at once sought to obtain from the Minister a statement of his intentions. The Minister replied that he had referred the decisions back in order that they could be reconsidered in the light of the statement on wages policy made by the Chancellor of the Exchequer to the National Joint Advisory Council in May. The Council thereupon sought an interview with the Prime Minister, which was at once granted. One week later the Minister of Labour informed the Economic Committee of the TUC that, while he could not withdraw the reference back, he would be prepared to expedite his consideration of the Wages Council's recommendations when they were resubmitted. In addition the Minister assured the TUC that he had no intention of interfering with the independence of Wages Councils, and he agreed to issue a statement to this effect for the future guidance of the Councils. Thus the Conservative Government when faced by the hostility of the TUC made a total retreat from its rather pathetic attempt to check an increase in the wages of the most weakly organized workers.

In the following year the Government made another general appeal to the unions to act with restraint, but the need to intervene had receded with the general check to the growth in demand produced by the Government's disinflationary economic policies, and the end of the Korean War boom. The volume of credit was reduced, the rate of interest was raised, and Government spending was cut. The net

[1] TUC Annual Report, 1952.
[2] Labour, November 1952.

effect of the various measures, coupled with a very severe recession in the textile industry brought on by other factors, was to increase unemployment to an average of over two per cent for the year. The impact of the change on the rate of increase in the aggregate wage-bill was such that it was only two-thirds of what it had been in 1951.

It might have been expected that the curb on wage increases and the rise in prices induced by the cutting of subsidies might well have provoked an outbreak of industrial unrest. The number of stoppages and working days lost did increase, but the fear that in the absence of a no-strike law the unions would be only too ready to seize an opportunity to embarrass a Conservative Government was not borne out by events. However, in 1954 the atmosphere grew more tense and there were whispers on both sides of industry that the time was approaching for a show-down. The Government were not prepared to permit a deterioration in the climate of industrial relations if that could be avoided, and they appointed Lord Justice Morris to preside over courts of inquiry which they established to avoid a major stoppage in the shipbuilding and engineering industries.

The reports of the Courts entered into dangerous territory when they suggested that there should be some authoritative and impartial body appointed to consider the complex and sometimes conflicting economic arguments; to form an opinion of the claims from the point of view of their impact upon the national economy and the ability of the country to maintain present standards, and to give advice and guidance as to broad policy and possible action. The members of the Courts were led to this conclusion when they were called upon to consider to what extent wage increases could be met from profits, the significance of an annual round of wage claims, and the extent to which a wage increase might provoke a general increase in production costs; also, in turn, how serious such a development would be from the point of view of the balance of payments.

The Government welcomed this suggestion and optimistically referred the question to the National Joint Advisory Council. But both sides of industry had their reservations and when the Government later presented a draft memorandum on the subject it was killed by the hostile attitude of the TUC. Rather than publish a completely emasculated document, which would have simply provided a target for the gibes of their critics, the Government withdrew its proposals.

The TUC was equally hostile to a proposal made by the Permanent Secretary of the Ministry of Labour in 1954 that all industries should make provision for arbitration as a final stage in the settlement of a dispute. This idea was warmly commended by sections of the Press and the Minister put the idea to the National Joint Advisory Council

for its consideration. The TUC caustically pointed out that provision
for arbitration in the last resort was no guarantee of good industrial
relations and they were uncompromisingly against any attempt to
compel the parties to industrial disputes to eschew strikes in favour
of arbitration. The Government again decided that discretion was the
best way of confronting intransigence, and no attempt was made to
re-launch the kite which, on its fall to earth, had been so uncere-
moniously trampled upon by the TUC.

The attitude of the TUC had been affected by the Government's
consistent rejection of its proposals on budgetary policy. Since 1951
the General Council had, year after year, urged the Government to
reduce the cost of living by increasing subsidies and reducing purchase
tax on consumer essentials, to increase taxation on distributed profits
and to encourage investment in essential industries and services by
discriminatory depreciation allowances.

In the opinion of the General Council and the delegates to Congress
the Government's policy of abolishing price controls, cutting subsidies and reducing direct taxation was not calculated to achieve 'a
favourable climate for price stability'. There was, stated the Council,
a widespread impression that the sacrifices necessary to overcome the
country's economic difficulties were being mainly borne by workpeople. Because of its profound disagreement with the economic
policy of the Government the General Council refused to sponsor the
circulation of the White Paper on the Economic Implications of Full
Employment,[1] published in 1956.

From the point of view of the interest of wage earners the TUC
had legitimate grounds for criticizing policies that were motivated
by desires to arrest the egalitarian trend in income distribution. The
net effect, however, of the Conservative Government's fiscal policy
has so far been more psychologically than economically reactionary.
Whatever the intention of the Government might have been, its
endeavours have resulted in a redistribution of income from the
higher to the lower paid groups on at least the same scale as happened
under the Labour Party. In spite of the substantial reductions in direct
taxes the proportions paid on real incomes equivalent to £2,000 a year
and over in 1947–48 were higher in 1956 than during the years between
1947 and 1951, when a Labour Government was in office.[2] However,
the proportion paid in tax on incomes below £2,000 a year has fallen
significantly. This paradoxical outcome of the efforts of the Government to relieve the higher income groups of some of their tax burden

[1] Cmd 9725.
[2] F. W. Paish, 'The Real Incidence of Personal Taxation', *Lloyds Bank Review*,
January 1957.

has been frustrated by the steep slope of the tax curve, combined with inflation, which has automatically pushed the top incomes into higher tax brackets.

The reduction of subsidies and the continuation of purchase tax have also to be taken into account before a fair assessment of the full effects of the Conservative Government's policy can be made. When the net effect of these changes on retail prices is measured it proves to be much less significant than might have been anticipated. About one-fifth of the average rise in prices since 1951 has been due to changes in subsidies and indirect taxes. Thus the price increases that have occurred have been caused to an overwhelming extent by the inflationary rise in money incomes and raw material costs, rather than by changes in taxation.

The Government's fiscal policy might be criticized on the grounds that larger budget surpluses would have reduced the inflationary pressure and thus slowed the rate of price increase down. It is when the TUC's suggestions are looked at from the point of view of remedying this weakness in the Government's economic policy that they are found to be inadequate. The proposals made by the General Council would undoubtedly have brought about a more equal distribution of income than ever before, but in the process they would have added considerably to the inflation, unless they had been accompanied by wage restraint. Without questioning the sincerity with which the General Council urged its proposals as an essential prerequisite to the adoption of wage restraint, it can be doubted whether in the inflationary conditions that would follow if they were accepted it would, at the same time, be possible to curb the demand for higher money incomes. A similar criticism may be brought to bear against the suggestion that more investment ought to be encouraged by tax incentives. This idea has much to commend it, but again the results would be inflationary if equivalent savings were not made elsewhere; in other words, a balance would have to be achieved by raising taxes or by increasing the size of undistributed profits at the expense of wages, salaries and dividends, or by attracting more private savings by a high rate of interest. In this respect attention must be drawn to the remarkable increase in net savings since 1952. After deducting the cost of depreciation total savings rose from £712 million in 1952 to £1,520 million in 1956, an increase of over 100 per cent. The most important source of this increase in savings was personal thrift and undistributed profits.[1]

[1] For a fuller account of this development see 'Savings and Investment in the United Kingdom', by F. W. Paish, *London and Cambridge Economic Bulletin*, December 1957.

It might well be asked why, if savings have increased at such a spectacular rate, there should have been a continuance of inflationary pressure. The answer is to be found in the simple fact that investment at home and abroad also rose during the same period by a very substantial amount. So that significant as was the rise in savings, it was not large enough to finance the expansion in fixed assets, stocks and overseas lending.[1] By this test it could certainly be argued that the economic policy of the Conservative Government had not been entirely successful, but suggestions for change must also satisfy the need to finance investment by an adequate flow of savings.

The Position of the Nationalized Industries

The responsibility of the Government in relation to the wage policy of the nationalized industries was a question left unanswered when the Labour Government embarked on its programme of public ownership. It is doubtful if serious thought was ever given to the implications of nationalization from the point of view of maintaining general economic stability, except in vague and general terms of expanding investment and raising wages. Since the nationalized industries were to be, to a defined extent, autonomous institutions, they were apparently to be left free to follow their own wage policies.

It soon became apparent that the Government could not entirely divest itself of responsibility for decisions affecting labour costs in nationalized industries. The decision of the National Coal Board to introduce a five-day week was only reached after behind-the-scenes pressures had been exerted which involved the Minister of Fuel and Power. But it was the railways which raised the problem in a manner which acutely embarrassed the Labour Government. In the summer of 1949, as the Government was desperately struggling to protect the value of the pound sterling, the National Union of Railwaymen threatened to bring the railway system to a complete halt unless its claims were granted. Since the position was bedevilled by the jealousies and hatreds between the railway unions, the Minister of Labour had little choice but to step in and take the issue out of the hands of the Railway Executive. It was, however, in 1951 that the railwaymen's organizations really exposed the weakness of a Government that could not afford to stand firm behind its economic policy.

Following a failure to agree on the demands of the unions a Court of Inquiry was established, but its recommendations were not acceptable, nor would the unions agree to a further improvement on them proposed by the Railway Executive. To avert a national railway strike the Government intervened and the Cabinet decided that the railway-

[1] Paish, *op. cit.*

men should be granted the increases which they demanded. The implications of this decision did not need pointing out to the unions and employers. By raising the five per cent increase, proposed by the Court of Inquiry and based upon 'the maximum amount which it is within the capacity of British Railways to pay', to 7½ per cent, the Government had given a lead which repudiated its policy of restraint. It had also destroyed the basis upon which its economic policy had previously been founded. As *The Economist* pointed out, the Government's policy had rested upon a middle way between open inflation and old-fashioned monetary compulsions to keep demand in check. Trade union restraint over wages, controls on prices and distribution and moderation in dividend increases had together kept the economy from the extremities of inflation, without the need of a financial discipline politically too harsh for the Labour Party.[1] What the railway settlement had done was to destroy this middle choice. If the Government could not resist the pressure of the unions, and wages were allowed to rise much faster than production, then the problem of inflation could only be tackled from the side of monetary supply, and sooner or later this would have to be faced.

The Conservatives were almost as reluctant as the Labour Party to use economic weapons to stop the inflation. They were afraid that they would be accused of creating mass unemployment and of deliberately seeking to crush the unions. In their turn they appointed as Minister of Labour a man in whom they knew the unions had confidence because they did not regard him as an ordinary Conservative politician. Every effort was made to avoid a head-on clash with the unions.

In 1953 the wages problem was again sharply dramatized by the determination of the railway unions to secure wage increases far greater than the bankrupt railways, or any principle of commercial accounting could possibly sustain without a reduction in services. The Minister of Labour had again intervened to prevent a strike and again the Transport Commission was compelled by the Government to raise its offer. Further claims led to the establishment of a Court of Inquiry, which reported in January 1955.[2] The Court ruled that the Transport Commission could not refuse to meet the demands of the unions on the grounds that to do so would violate the injunction in the Transport Act, which calls upon the Commission to balance revenue and expenditure 'taking one year with another'. The Court held that the nation had provided by statute that there should be a nationalized system of railway transport, and, therefore, 'having

[1] *The Economist*, March 3, 1951.
[2] Cmd 9372.

willed the end, the nation must will the means'.[1] Thus an official body rules, in effect, that the railwaymen, because they were employed by a nationalized industry, were, for that reason alone, entitled to the rates of pay in force in other industries.

Twice the Transport Commission was thus compelled by the Govenment to settle claims at levels that would have led any private enterprise to go out of business. In each case the settlement established a pattern which was followed by other industries. In these circumstances it was, perhaps, only to be expected that in 1956 the Transport Commission would have little stomach for resistance and would settle with as little delay as possible. But considering that the Commission had an accumulated deficit of £40 million its offer of a seven per cent increase came as a surprise. It may well have been the hope of the Commission that the unions would then give the industry a little longer breathing space to recoup some of the increase it had incurred in labour costs. If this were the motive it was doomed to failure, since the National Union of Railwaymen was not yet satisfied that workers on the railways were receiving a fair wage. In the autumn of 1956 a further ten per cent was demanded. The Commission offered to meet this claim by increasing all wages by three per cent. This proposal was rejected and eventually, in the face of another strike threat, five per cent was conceded in March 1957. In October 1957 the National Union of Railwaymen submitted a new claim for a ten per cent wage increase, a forty-hour week and an additional week's holiday with pay. In the meantime the Government had stiffened its economic policy and the claim for an increase in railwaymen's wages had become once again a touchstone of future developments.

The Evolution of the Government's Policy
The growing militancy of the unions and the rising level of wage costs reached a culminating point when, in March 1957, 200,000 shipyard and 600,000 engineering workers came out on strike in support of their claim for a ten per cent increase in wages. The employers were prepared to concede a five per cent advance, but this did not meet with the approval of the unions. Following the intervention of the Government a Court of Inquiry was set up. In the event the Court proposed that wages should be increased by 11s with certain conditions, or 8s 6d without conditions. But the aspect of the Report which aroused most interest was the suggestion that an authoritative and impartial body should be established to consider the wider economic problems involved in the determination of wages, costs and prices.

[1] Cmd 9352. See also 'Wages on the Railways', by B. C. Roberts, *Political Quarterly*, April–June 1955.

The deteriorating economic situation convinced the Government that it should adopt the recommendation of the Court, and it established a Council on Prices, Productivity and Incomes. But before the Council could start work the Government was compelled to take emergency action to protect the value of the pound. The Bank Rate was raised to seven per cent; the rate of capital expenditure in the public sector, it was announced, would be kept at the 1957 level for the next two years; in the private sector bank, advances were to be limited in 1958 to the level of 1957.

The measures introduced by the Government were severely criticized by the trade unions. The leader of the Transport and General Workers' Union, proposing a motion at the Trades Union Congress which rejected wage restraint in any form, described the Council on Prices, Productivity and Incomes, as 'not realistic'. The burden of the union leaders' complaint was that it was unfair to curb wages by raising the Bank Rate and by curtailing the supply of money. An implication of the attack on the economic policy of the Conservative Party was that under a future Labour Government the unions would be prepared to accept wage restraint. In spite of the fact that price controls, subsidies and a low rate of interest had manifestly failed to avert a series of acute economic crises the faith of the unions in this approach to the economic problem has remained undimmed. Since all the evidence points to the impossibility of preventing inflation by administrative means, it may be doubted whether the unions will in the future be either any more able or willing to avoid pushing wages up faster than the growth in output than they have been in the past. A Labour Government may well inspire good intentions, but past experience does not give much cause to believe that the behaviour of the unions will be fundamentally different from what it has been under the Conservatives. Indeed, if it were to be different it would mean that the unions had ceased to regard the securing of higher wages as their basic function.

The determination of the Conservative Government not to float off further wage increases by an expansion of credit was emphasized by the Chancellor of the Exchequer and the Minister of Labour at the opening of Parliament after the 1957 summer recess. But it was the decision of the Government not to allow an agreement by the Whitley Council, responsible for the settlement of wages of clerical and other employees of the National Health Service below £1,200 a year, to raise the incomes of these grades by three per cent, which aroused the greatest indignation. This decision was apparently based on the belief that the Government should set the example it was calling upon other employers to follow, but it must be regarded as maladroit. It gave the impression that the Government was prepared to intervene directly in the fixing of wages. This was unfortunate, since the Government had no intention of freezing wages and it had only power to pursue a wage policy that would be certainly arbitrary and unjust. It could hardly be expected that ten years of inflation could be brought to an end overnight, and if wage increases were to be eased down to an overall increase of two or three per cent a year, much would have been achieved.

Unfortunately the impression was created by the Government that a 'showdown' with the unions might be desired by some at least of its members. It is certain that none of the responsible leaders of the trade unions wanted to see a period of massive industrial unrest; most of them were well aware that in a head-on conflict they were bound to come off far worse than the Government. Encouraged, however, by Labour politicians, the union leaders made few attempts to adapt their policy to the economic situation; they simply continued to press for far higher wages than the actual economic situation could stand on any rational consideration. By switching their attention from wage claims to other important issues, such as redundancy compensation, pensions, supplementary sickness payments and other fringe benefits, the unions might well have been able to register important and socially desirable gains, without at the same time adding as much to inflationary pressure as a wage claim. It is not difficult to explain why British unions have looked upon collective bargaining almost entirely in the narrow setting of wage increases. They have been greatly influenced by two factors; the centralized character of the collective bargaining process, and the adoption of a socialist ideology, with a close attachment to the Labour Party.

The centralization of collective bargaining has focused the attention of the unions on the negotiation of basic industry-wide wage rates. Local agreements are permitted, and many of them are negotiated, but the principal concern of the union leaders is the basic agreement. Since fringe benefits can only be negotiated to a very limited extent on an industry-wide basis, they do not, and cannot, figure prominently in national agreements. If attention is to be switched from wages to fringe benefits, then a change of emphasis in negotiations is involved and this is extremely difficult to achieve when the structure, administration and leadership of the unions is geared in the first place to the determination of issues at the national level.

The institutional rigidity of British Labour organizations is reinforced by the ideological attitude of the active members of the unions, and their attachment to the Labour Party. Since it is a socialist objective to centralize the provision of social security in the hands of the state, the unions have been reluctant to take steps which deviate from this goal. This is why they have been slow to demand that employers should provide manual workers with the supplementary unemployment benefit, sickness schemes and pension programmes which are widely available to clerical, technical and managerial employees. Where such arrangements have been extended to wage earners it has generally been at the initiative of the employer, not of the union.

The reluctance of the unions to face fully the economic and social problems posed by the task of maintaining full employment without inflation, is another aspect of the confusion created by the difficulty of reconciling a socialist ideology with a basically pragmatic and liberal pattern of behaviour.

The dilemma which confronts the unions is that they exist to protect and promote the interests of their members by industrial and political action, whatever Government may be in office. But, at the same time, many of the leaders of the unions are against the private enterprise system and wish to replace it by a fully planned economy and the nationalization of all industry. Thus, in their attitude to economic problems, the unions are torn between conflicting ideological points of view.

The belief, widely held by the active members of trade unions, that profits are immoral, has made it difficult for them to undertake a rational consideration of the social and economic problems of a basically private enterprise economy, under conditions of full employment. The hard facts of the situation have often been obscured by a welter of political slogans which have contributed little towards an understanding of the fundamental issues.

The Conservative Government was criticized by the unions for tackling inflation by way of raising the Bank Rate and curbing the supply of money. As an alternative the unions would, apparently, have preferred the reintroduction of price controls, building licensing, import controls and higher taxes on profits and dividends. These policies would not, however, have been successful, as previous experience has amply demonstrated, without the application of a curb to the creation of excessive money incomes. It would have been necessary to prevent wages and salaries from rising faster than output, if price controls were not to be circumvented by the pressure of demand. But would the unions be prepared to accept a national wages policy as the inevitable concomitant of a general policy of controls?

This question has only to be asked to be answered by past experience: what a previous Labour Government failed to do, a Conservative Government would find impossible; and a future Labour Government is hardly likely to win support for the revival of a regimented system which includes controls over wages as well as prices, over labour as well as capital.

If the unions will not accept direct controls over their wage bargaining activities then the Government of the day, from whatever party it may be drawn, when faced by inflation has no alternative but to pursue a monetary and fiscal policy fundamentally similar to that adopted in September 1957 by the Conservatives, if it wishes to prevent the continuance of price rises and a further devaluation of the pound. A Labour Government may well choose to supplement its monetary and fiscal policies with certain physical controls and these would undoubtedly help to check an inflationary tendency, but over any long-run period it would be impossible to rely on the effectiveness of controls if the pressure of demand was allowed to continue to build up.

It is not recognized by many trade unionists that the 'planned' economy for which they often ask is incompatible with free collective bargaining. If industry were to be entirely publicly owned and the economy directed according to some central plan, it is obvious that wages could not be left free to be decided by collective bargaining. The trade unions could not be permitted to claim the right to behave as they chose and at the same time deny the same rights to others. Collective bargaining requires two sides and both sides must be free to arrive at their decisions in the light of an independent judgment of the consequences. If the context in which the decisions were taken was not one in which responsibility rested with the unions and the enterprises concerned, every decision would inevitably beome a political issue. Events in nationalized industries and the public service have already indicated how easily this occurs. It is difficult to believe that the consequences that would follow from making wage decisions a political football would be any less dangerous to economic stability and social welfare than those that follow from free collective bargaining in a market economy. Sooner or later the unions must recognize that they have to choose whether they want a completely regulated economy, or one in which to a large extent independent employers and unions can autonomously decide, within the context of economic and social forces at work, what is the best solution to their needs. The evidence as to what the choice will ultimately be points most strongly in one direction and that is away from public ownership, central direction and total planning, to the maintenance of a pluralistic economic and social system. It is likely that another period of Labour Government will enable the unions to decide what are the limits of nationalization, physical controls and the boundaries of freedom and responsibility in the field of wage determination.

CHAPTER 11

The Rational Approach
to Wages Policy

A centralized system of wage controls has been advocated on three grounds: (1) that only by this means can trade unions be prevented from exerting such pressure, under full employment, as inevitably to bring about an inflationary increase in costs and prices; (2) that only by this means can the structure of wages be adapted so as to fulfil the essential role of allocating resources; (3) that only by this means can wages be determined in accordance with principles of justice.

Whatever in theory might be said in favour of a centralized system of wage controls, it cannot be said that those examined in the previous chapters have succeeded in preventing inflation. Although there are considerable differences in historical traditions, economic circumstances and institutional arrangements, it is possible to draw certain general conclusions from the experience gained in these experiments, which explains why they have failed to achieve their primary objective.

The Impulse to Inflation

The inflation of the past two decades had its genesis in war; in the period of conflict there was built up an excessive supply of relatively liquid assets and a massive back-log of unsatisfied demand. Here, then, was fuel for inflation ready to hand. No Government was in a position to quench the flames easily by shutting off the fuel supply, but most Governments actually made the situation worse. In their natural anxiety to maintain full employment and to advance economic security they shunned policies which in the past had been associated with depression and which had been the subject of the most bitter intellectual battles. The net result was that the authorities added directly to the inflation by their own excessive expenditure; and they failed to make private saving more attractive than spending at a time when there were inadequate resources available to meet the existing level of demand. Thus the post-war inflation got off to a good start, and it therefore became more difficult than might otherwise have been the case to hold it in check as time went on.

Governments in the post-war years were also concerned to achieve other widely desired ends, as well as full employment. They had large arrears in investment to overtake; they had huge defence commitments to meet; in most cases an adverse balance of payments had to be corrected and overseas capital investments had to be re-stored by increasing exports; in addition a vast expansion of social welfare was a *sine qua non* of political survival.

The problem which faced every Government was to finance this formidable programme by methods which would avoid creating an inflationary situation. This task was made much more difficult by the constant endeavour of every section of the community to increase its personal income and to raise its standards of living as rapidly as possible. The principal instrument chosen by most Governments to control the economic situation with which they were faced was the Budget.

If total outlays could be balanced by taxation and savings and a surplus achieved on the balance of payments account all would be well. There need be no fear of inflation and so long as the economy was growing there would be the possibility of continuously raising real income. Unfortunately, however, the pressure of the various demands led to larger outlays than could be financed without inflation and recurring balance of payments crises.

The Cost-Push Theory of Inflation

In these circumstances wage changes came to be looked upon as a key item, not because wage earners desired higher incomes more avidly than salary earners and those in receipt of fees, rent, interest, dividends and profits, but because wages account for over forty per cent of total personal income. Since wages are also a prime cost, any change is bound to be felt immediately on the cost of production and, therefore, may quickly influence other aspects of the economy. Wages per worker in British manufacturing industry rose by seventy-three per cent from 1948 to 1956, whilst total labour costs per unit of output went up by forty-two per cent.

Here, then, it would seem, was the root cause of the inflationary spiral, wages rising faster than output, leading to an increase in labour costs that is passed on to the consumer in the form of higher prices.[1] Since the higher wages have usually been conceded by employers following demands made upon them by trade unions, the conclusion that the whole problem has its origins in trade union pressure appears irresistible. It is, then, a simple step to the proposition that the only solution is to substitute some other system of wage determination for

[1] See Table 23, chapter 10.

L

free collective bargaining in order to restrict wage increases to the productive capacity of the economy.

The simple analysis on which this conclusion is based proves on closer examination to be an inadequate explanation of inflation. Wage increases are not necessarily inflationary, since a rise in costs followed by a rise in prices will check the increase in demand. If, however, the supply of money is increased the rise in wages and prices will not remain at a new equilibrium, because the level of demand will be raised a stage further. It is his belief that increases in costs caused by wage rises are bound to induce the authorities to increase the supply of money that has led Professor Hicks to suggest that our modern economy is on a 'Labour Standard'. The decision, however, to increase the supply of money is not, it should be noted, an automatic consequence of wage increases. It is, in fact, a deliberate act of policy; in other words it is a political rather than an economic decision which makes a rise in wage costs have an inflationary instead of a deflationary effect.

It is argued, however, that wage increases can be an autonomous source of inflation requiring no act of money creation to finance a rising spiral of wages and prices. The figures of money supply in both Britain and America, in the past few years, may to some extent be cited as evidence that simply to control the quantity of money will not be enough to check an excessive rise in the level of effective demand. In the United States the money supply, as Table 24 shows, was increased in the past four years by no more than the output of goods and services. In Britain the total money supply has since 1950 almost certainly been held down below the growth in output.

TABLE 24
Percentage Increase in the Supply of Money

	UK	US		UK	US
1950	2	6	1954	3	3
1951	2	6	1955	–	3
1952	–	4	1956	1	3
1953	3	2			

What these figures do not show is the very considerable increase in the use to which the stocks of money have been put. Until 1949 the rate at which bank deposits were being turned over was roughly two-thirds of the 1938 rate. But since 1952 there has been a remarkable increase in the rate of turnover; it has been calculated that it was twenty-five per cent higher in 1956 than it had been in 1938. The income velocity of money can also be measured by dividing the average level of balances on current account into the gross national product. The result shows an increase of over fifty per cent since

1950.[1] In the United States the supply of money has been so actively used as to finance an expansion of goods and services three or four times larger than the increase in the quantity of money.[2] A further aspect of the activization of money in Britain has been the substantial increase in the currency note issue, which between 1951 and 1956 expanded by two and a half times as much as real output.

Here, then, we have the reason why the rise in wage costs and final prices has not automatically brought the inflation to an end. The transfer from idle to active balances and the increase in the turnover of deposits and cash in circulation has financed the continuance of inflation by building up the level of demand to meet each new price level. In other words, cost-inflation has only continued by turning into demand inflation. There is, however, no constant relationship between changes in wages and prices and the velocity of circulation or monetary supply. Whether or not the money is forthcoming to finance a constantly rising level of demand in the face of an ever-rising price level is ultimately a matter of decision by the authorities. The extent to which money is activated is a function of the rate of interest and the expectations of businessmen and can be checked by an appropriate monetary policy; it can also be checked by a variety of administrative controls.

If the above analysis is correct it is obvious that wage increases have played an important part in the chain of events which we call inflation. It is necessary, however, before arriving at conclusions as to the appropriate policy to follow to maintain economic stability, to inquire to what extent wage increases have been responsible for initiating the process. From the examination of the experience of various countries there is good reason to believe that the trade unions have by no means been the main culprits.

In each of the countries examined, the phenomenon which is described by the Swedes as the 'wage drift' has made its appearance. The level of wages set by the institutional machinery has generally been below the market equilibrium. This can be seen from the difference between the level of wage rates negotiated and the actual earnings received by workers. The demand for labour has been such that employers have been ready and able to pay more than was required by their agreements with trade unions to recruit and maintain a supply of labour to meet their needs.

It might be suggested that since the structure of earnings is based upon a foundation of wage rates, the upward drift in earnings is, therefore, simply a reflection of the upward movement of the basic

[1] *Midland Bank Review*, November 1957.
[2] *New York Times*, August 6, 1957.

L*

wage. There is certainly a connection between changes in wage rates and changes in earnings; as wage rates have been pushed up by the pressure of the unions, they have lifted the level of earnings to a higher point, but the rate of change in earnings has not been identical with the rate of change in wage rates. The statistics of wages in the various countries show that both wage rates and earnings are affected by the demand for labour, but earnings have been affected to a greater extent. It is likely that the gap between wage rates and earnings, which is largely accounted for by overtime, payment by results schemes, 'plus rates' and changes in the employment structure, would be greatly narrowed if unemployment were to rise, even if it did not rise to anything approaching the pre-war level.

Since the fact that employers are willing to pay for the labour they require is reflected in earnings the problem will not be solved by holding wages down. From the experience of the countries examined it can be stated categorically that a national wage policy will not, in a democratic country, succeed in keeping wages down in the face of excess demand. It is useless to attempt to cure inflation by preventing the unions from negotiating higher wages if these are warranted by the profits that employers are making. If the unions are not able to push wages up to the market level then they will be pulled up by employers in their endeavour to satisfy their demand for labour.

The inflationary rise in incomes might, therefore, be ascribed to over-easily earned profits, rather than to over-strong trade unions. Thus, in a sense, the union leaders are right to point to high profits as a principal cause of inflation, but for the wrong reasons. If profits were more difficult to earn and competition in the product market was more vigorous, employers would be more reluctant than they have been in recent years to put wages up. A solution to the problem of the wage-price spiral may then be properly seen in terms of preventing profits from rising too quickly.

It therefore becomes an essential condition of a successful wage policy that there should be no demand inflation. If there is no demand inflation then cost inflation must soon peter out. If this is so, it may be asked why, from the point of view of preventing inflation, a national wages policy should be necessary. The answer must clearly be that a national wages policy is redundant if the aggregate level of demand is not permitted to exceed that level required to maintain full, but not over-full employment.

Curbing Excess Demand
The problem then becomes one of preventing the generation of excess demand by methods other than the administrative control of

wages. The level of demand will be primarily influenced by the rate of investment in the public and private sectors and by the rate of consumption. Any policy designed to control the aggregate level of demand must see that total expenditure on these items does not exceed the resources available. The most simple way of ensuring that the level of demand does not rise too rapidly is to maintain a strict control of the credit system. The techniques by which it is possible to prevent the rate of credit expansion and the velocity of circulation from exceeding desirable limits are well known and it is not essential that they should be discussed here in detail.

The obligation which rests upon the Government is to see that its own expenditure does not exceed a level which can be financed without creating an inflationary expansion of credits. It is, however, feared by some economists that the use of credit controls, the rate of interest and the control of the rate of capital expenditure in the public sector will have adverse economic effects. This fear is in part a psychological hangover from the struggle waged against the *laissez-faire* economists of the past, who refused to see that full employment could be established by deliberate actions on the part of the State. It is also due to a belief that a cut in demand will not prevent unions from continuing to push up wages and, therefore, that it will merely result in reducing urgently required capital developments and in curbing production. Some economists have, indeed, argued that to cut demand might only succeed in making the inflationary situation worse, since it would reduce output without proportionately reducing demand.

It may well be true that an attack on inflation by curtailing the supply of credit and capital expenditure will have the immediate effect of checking output. This did, in fact, happen in 1952 and it seems to have happened in 1956; it has also happened in other countries. Unfortunately, this price may inevitably have to be paid to achieve stability. It does not follow, however, once a stable equilibrium has been achieved, that production will remain stationary; there is no logical reason why it should not go on rising after the initial deflationary shock to a system geared to inflation has been overcome and once the re-allocation of resources has been achieved.

It is possible that the checking of an inflation by curtailing demand will lead to a rise in unemployment from the low average of 1.5 per cent which has prevailed since 1948. Again, however, it does not follow that unemployment need be kept permanently much higher than this average, but in order to keep a low average level of unemployment with economic stability it will certainly be necessary to allow swings about the average. That is to say, unemployment will have to go up as well as down. It is vitally important that this should be recognized, since otherwise, as the Swedish trade unions have explicitly pointed out, it will be impossible to have price stability with full employment.[1] This is not a plea for mass unemployment, but simply a recognition that a complex economy cannot be steered like a baby car. The level of unemployment will remain as the principal indicator of the economic health of the nation, but we must not get into a panic when the body economic reacts to dangerous poisons by adjustments in the employment temperature. If we pursue the right treatment we will bring it back to normal without reaching a state of crisis.

There are those who consider that it is not necessary to allow unemployment to rise at all in any circumstances. If, they argue, physical controls are used, it will not be necessary to permit unemployment to rise, and the evil consequences to the public purse of raising the interest charges on the national debt and local authority borrowing will be avoided.

Undoubtedly a high rate of interest has grave disadvantages, but as one among other instruments of policy it has its special virtues. It avoids the serious problem of administering a whole battery of complex controls, which are often clumsy, inefficient and unjust in their effect. Nevertheless, just as the rate of interest has a function, so too have physical controls in particular circumstances. It may in certain circumstances be preferable to exercise a control over, say, building, over capital issues, over imports, rather than to rely entirely on a high interest rate to curb borrowing and check a decline in the gold and dollar reserves.

What is difficult to excuse is the pursuit of mutually incompatible policies. Both the Labour and Conservative Governments have been guilty in this respect. During the Labour Government's tenure of office, it continually created too much demand by its pursuit of a cheap money policy along with excessive Government expenditure. It then tried to cope with the consequences by various controls and by appealing to the unions to exercise wage restraint. In these circumstances the task of the unions was impossible and they inevitably let the Labour Government down. When the Conservatives came into office they raised interest rates, but they continued to generate an excessive level of demand, by their spending and borrowing policy. Through their fear of the wrath of the unions and their political concern to avoid being labelled the party of unemployment, they did not effectively discourage the nationalized industries and the private sector from raising wages far faster than productivity was rising. In

[1] See page 166.

this respect the record of events in Britain since 1950 is to be contrasted with events in Germany, where productivity has not been consistently outstripped by wage increases.

A sound economic policy clearly requires the use of budgetary, monetary and physical controls. Within the broad framework of economic policy it should be left to the unions and the employers to work out the appropriate wage levels by collective negotiation. It is only by the pursuit of an economic policy that keeps aggregate demand in line with available resources that free collective bargaining can be maintained without wage controls or inflation. The unions must make up their minds what they want. Do they want a controlled economy in which the right of collective bargaining is taken over by the state? If they do not want to lose their wage negotiating function then they must accept the limitation of aggregate demand. The alternative is the continuance of inflation, bringing with it the destruction of savings and pensions, and the gradual weakening of Britain's economic strength by recurrent economic crises which will remorselessly reduce the value of the pound.

If aggregate demand is kept at the appropriate level to maintain full, but not over-full employment, then if the unions push up wages too fast they will merely succeed in creating additional unemployment. The responsibility upon their shoulders is that they should not seek to obtain wage increases which outpace by far the rise in production. Whilst it is futile to expect trade unions to exercise wage restraint in the face of rising profits and a level of demand that obviously permits costs to be passed on without affecting employment, it is unlikely that they will push their claims to the extent of seriously affecting the numbers employed. It must be stressed that it is not required of the unions that they should cease to seek higher wages; it is, in fact, important that they should continue to press for wage increases, since the continuous pressure for higher real incomes is one of the principal dynamic factors in a modern industrial society. Is it asking for the impossible to state that the unions must carry the responsibility of exercising such pressure as will contribute towards the securing of a higher standard of living, without pressing so hard as to cause massive industrial unrest, or too much unemployment? Given the determination of the general level of demand by the proper exercise of Government economic policy, the policy of the unions will be determined within an area bounded by the pressure of the members for higher incomes, the cost of striking, the cost of causing unemployment, and the amount of the gross product the employers are able and willing to concede.[1]

[1] A strike may be a primitive way to settle an issue which in theory should be

It might be objected that much more is being asked of the unions than is asked of employers. But this is not so. There is no likelihood of the employers being able to make exorbitant profits in the circumstances outlined. In fact, employers will find the job of profit-making far more difficult than has been the case in the years of inflation. They will not be able gaily to pass on any increase in costs in higher prices; they will have to absorb higher costs by greater efficiency. The net effect, therefore, will not be to benefit the receivers of dividends at the expense of other income groups. Another social reason for curbing inflation is that it will trim the capital gains that have been a feature of inflation; since profits will be harder to earn there will be no dramatic stock exchange boom. Indeed, as inflation is brought under control, there is likely to be a far greater fall in inflated capital values than would ever be skimmed off by any politically feasible capital gains tax.

It would be possible for British trade unions to follow the example of the American unions and negotiate long-term agreements, say for five years, with an automatic annual increase based on productivity. The difficulty inherent in a policy of this type is that productivity rises very much more quickly in the manufacturing and processing industries than in services. If, therefore, the full rate of productivity increase is taken out of the former sector of the economy, the only way in which commensurate wage increases could be granted for services would be by way of price increases. An alternative, but one requiring a much more subtle approach, would be to base the rate of wage increase on the average rate of increase in the real national product. It would then follow that those sectors of industry with a more than average gain in productivity would have to lower their prices by an amount equal to the difference between their own output and the average. In this way they would pass on their gains to the other sectors of the economy and all would participate. It would, in theory, be possible to work out all the complications of such a policy, but in practice it would be impossible to achieve more than the roughest justice. It is, therefore, likely, even when the economy is running at a less feverish heat than has been the case in the post-war years, that there will still be a tendency for service costs and prices to rise, simply because it is unlikely that labour in the manufacturing

susceptible to rational decision, but we must allow for human beings behaving irrationally even in our scientifically dominated society. It may calm the fears of those who see in strikes an evil only a little less than war to quote the Conservative Minister of Labour, Mr Iain Macleod, who stated that in 1956 'we lost through industrial disputes no more than fifty minutes for every worker engaged in industry. We lost through industrial accidents eight hours, and through sickness 100 hours.' *The Times*, October 31, 1957.

sector will be induced to keep its demands low enough to avoid this situation. This conclusion rests, however, on the assumption that sufficient income will be generated to allow the prices of services to rise without creating unemployment. In other words, it is likely, even after the excessive demand of recent years has been squeezed out, that some slight creep in the average price level will be inevitable if employment is maintained at a high level. If the rise in prices can be kept down to, say, between one and two per cent per annum, instead of the five to six per cent in the post-war decade, this creep will be a relatively small price to pay for a high and stable level of employment.

Since there is a possibility that some increase in unemployment may be caused in bringing an inflationary situation under control it is essential that everything should be done to protect the interests of those displaced. The most important step is to see that unemployment benefit is raised to a proper level. The position in Britain for many years has been that unemployment benefit has fallen to the absurdly low level of less than forty per cent of average earnings. This contrasts with the much higher percentage before the war and with the level of unemployment payments made in America. It is true that unemployment benefit is frequently supplemented by national assistance, but this is no substitute for an adequate level of unemployment pay.

In this connection there is probably considerable scope for the development, in Britain, of something akin to the idea of the guaranteed wage which was pioneered in the United States, and developed on a major scale by the United Automobile Workers' Union. The advantage of this kind of arrangement lies not only in the provision of more adequate social security, but in that it may well have some disinflationary effect. To the extent that the funding of the contributions amounts to net saving, the allocation of a larger amount of income for the purpose of guaranteeing at least two-thirds of a worker's average earnings for a certain time period, would be an economic advantage.

Wage Structure and National Wage Policy
The aggregate level of wages is not the only aspect of wage determination that has been called in question under full employment.The structure of wages that has emerged has been widely criticized as failing to reflect the needs of social, economic and industrial circumstances. It has been suggested that inappropriate differentials are maintained because they are determined by the power of sectional interests rather than by objective criteria. There can be no doubt that present wage structures are often unsatisfactory from the point of

view of encouraging maximum productivity, adequate mobility, greater responsibility and better industrial relations. From what direction is improvement to come? By means of further centralization, as desired by some critics, or by a change in collective bargaining in the opposite direction?

Many people feel that wage differentials have been narrowed too much and that Britain's economic health would benefit if they were widened. During the past forty years the difference between the wage rates paid to unskilled and skilled workers has been halved in many industries. Clerical and supervisory staffs used to enjoy considerable advantages over wage earners, in income and working conditions, but the difference in wages, holidays with pay, pension and sickness provisions has been greatly reduced. There has also been a substantial reduction of inter-industry wage differentials since 1939.

During the past few years there has been a growing tendency, on both sides of industry, to question the wisdom of reducing the difference in wage rates still further. There is, in fact, evidence indicating that a substantial revolt against the principle of uniformity has taken place in the past few years. Acute conflict has occurred in the printing industry and on the railways over the question of widening differentials. In a number of other industries, including engineering, recent wage claims have been made on a percentage basis. Perhaps the most significant evidence that the wage rate structure is unbalanced is the spread of actual earnings. The nationally agreed wage rate, more often than not, bears little relation to the wages that a man earns. In order to obtain the labour that they have required, employers have entered into local agreements with shop stewards, or on their own initiative have increased wages to levels indicated by conditions in their own labour market. Since the Ministry of Labour does not publish occupational earnings figures it is difficult to assess the changes that have occurred, but there can be little doubt that the pattern of actual money payments has reflected the real pressures in the labour market far more accurately than the structure of nationally negotiated money wage rates.

A similar situation has prevailed in Holland, Sweden and Australia, where determined efforts have been made to establish and enforce policies designed to reduce differentials to a minimum. What has become clear, however, is that wage structures, whether determined by collective bargaining or legal regulation, are not likely to prove satisfactory if established by a centralized body at the national level. Local labour markets are far more important than the advocates of national wage policies have assumed. This fact ought to be taken into account when wage policy is under consideration. It means that unions should pay far more attention to plant wage agreements than they have in the past.

Great efforts have been made by the European Productivity Agency and by the TUC Production Department to bring home to trade unions what they might achieve for their members by negotiating effective plant wage agreements. Drastic revisions of wage structures are often necessary if the best is to be obtained from new techniques and methods and if a fair reward is to go to their operators. This type of problem cannot be handled by a centralized national body; it must be resolved on the spot by careful study and skilled negotiation. A certain degree of guidance may come from the centre, but each case should be tackled on its merits and the solution tailored to fit the situation. This approach means that unions muct turn their gaze from the centre to the periphery, if a new pattern of differentials, new ways of rewarding merit, efficiency and experience are to be found to meet the needs of an age of automation.

National Wage Policy and Social Justice
Intimately bound up with the economic aspects of wage determination, whether considered from the point of view of the total wage bill or of relative wage levels, is the question of justice. It is impossible to disentangle notions of fairness from wage determination, since workers, like members of other groups in the community, are moved to action by feelings of injustice. But, because people are stimulated by conceptions of justice, it does not follow that equality is the sole criterion, as many of the exponents of a national wages policy seem to think. Greater equality in the distribution of the national income might be more just; but it is quite impossible to say what proportion of the national income should, in justice, go to wage earners, since there is no absolute standard by which such a judgment could be made. In practice, what is likely to happen is that attention will be paid to what in fact has been the distribution of the national income in the past. Those groups which find that they are not securing as large a share as previously will, it is generally found, claim that the past distribution was fair and that the change that has occurred is unfair. Those who have benefited will usually argue that it would be unfair to regard a previous state of affairs as immutable and that the change is only right and proper when considered from the point of view of justice. Any attempt to manipulate the shares of the national income going to particular groups by means of a deliberate policy decided upon by reference to some abstract conception of justice would almost certainly arouse tremendous distrust and conflict of views. The difficulty of obtaining agreement on an issue of this kind

was well illustrated when the Social and Economic Council of the Netherlands tried to grapple with a claim by the unions that the workers' share in the national income had declined.[1]

The task of fixing wage and salary differentials on the basis of justice rather than as a result of the pushes and pulls of the labour market would be equally insuperable. It is not enough to draw up a wages schedule based on an elaborate system of job evaluation as suggested by some advocates of a national wages policy.[2] Justice is not simply a matter of relating wages to job content. Wage earners include in their notions of a fair wage not only that an allowance should be made for differences in skill, effort and responsibility, but also that an opportunity should be given to take advantage of a favourable market situation. The fact that it might not be possible to square these two different approaches to the problem is something that may trouble the academic moralist, but not the wage earner himself. There can be no doubt, judging from behaviour, that preference lies with a wages structure that is determined by tradition, the freedom to bargain and the freedom to change jobs, rather than with a wages structure determined by a rigid formula.

The Essentials of a National Wage Policy

The conclusion at which we inescapably arrive is that a centralized system of wage controls is ill-fitted to cope with the complex problems of a modern industrial economy. Some form of regulation is indispensable, but a condition of a successful wage policy is that it should run in harmony with the broad trends which are set by the economic forces at work in the market. This does not mean that sociological factors can be ignored, but rather that it is impossible to develop a satisfactory wage policy based on notions which run counter to such fundamental factors as the supply of and demand for labour, both in general and in particular.

Whilst the growth of trade unionism and the development of a complex system of industrial relations has so far tended to work with rather than against the market, it is obvious that in some respects the result has been to inhibit necessary change. It may, for example, be doubted whether the degree of emphasis placed upon national industry-wide wage rates is, under conditions of full employment, either necessary or desirable from an economic or from an institutional point of view. The negotiation of wage rates on this basis inevitably makes a wage dispute a symbolic clash between 'class' interests. If inflation is to be avoided and the economic and social

[1] See page 124.
[2] C. A. Lidbury, *A National Wages Policy* (1947).

needs of the community are to be properly met, wages ought not to be a major political issue. If they become a focal point upon which political conflict centres then there is the very real danger that irreparable harm will be done to social and economic stability. In a sense it is, of course, impossible to keep wages out of politics, since real wages will be affected by the Government's economic policy. It is important, however, that the process of wage setting should be as autonomous as possible within the broader framework of a general economic policy. The smaller the unit responsible for the determination of any particular wage, the more decentralized the process of wage setting will be, and, therefore, the smaller will be the likelihood that any particular wage decision will involve an economic and political crisis.

The arguments against breaking down the present structure of collective bargaining are twofold, and they are advanced from opposite points of view. The first argument comes from those who recognize that the present system of national bargaining is complex and inevitably slow. The failure of wage rates to rise as fast as earnings is attributed to the time lags that are built into the present system. It is also noted that under a system of industry-wide bargaining the rate set will usually be below that which could be paid by the more efficient firms. There is, therefore, the fear that to decentralize collective bargaining would enhance the inflationary danger, since wage rates would respond more rapidly than in the past to the pressure of demand.

From the side of the unions, employers and Ministry of Labour officials, opposition is based upon tradition and vested interests. It is feared by the unions that to break down the present structure of collective bargaining would expose them to the power of the employers should there be a fall in the general level of demand for labour. This point of view is based upon the experience out of which industry-wide bargaining developed, but it may be questioned whether policies designed to meet problems of unemployment are the best that can be devised to meet the very different problems of full employment. Unions are also afraid of the decentralization of bargaining because of the effect that it might have on their organization. It would inevitably involve some devolution of authority, and in the case of some unions, this could possibly lead to a realignment of the internal distribution of power and might even result in the establishment of breakaway organizations. These fears need not come to pass if the problem of less centralized bargaining were faced squarely. Far better service would have to be given to local officers than is common today and communications would have to be vastly improved. From the point of view of union vitality the decentralization of bargaining could have a very beneficial effect.

It is precisely the fear that decentralized bargaining would lead to a more effective use of the lever technique that leads employers to prefer the present system. They think that a less centralized system would expose them to pressures which are now taken by their associations, and they are glad, as in other spheres, to avoid competitive pressures wherever this is possible.

It would be foolish to advocate the breaking up of every existing bargaining unit. There is clearly need to retain Wages Councils, in order to protect the interests of weakly organized workers, though this need is perhaps not as great as unions think. Indeed, it could be strongly argued that many Wages Council industries are still badly organized because they have Wages Councils. Many other collective bargaining arrangements probably work reasonably well, but there are some that clearly do not fulfil a useful purpose. The most obvious case for revision is in the so-called 'engineering' industry. This is not one industry, but many, and the present system of collective bargaining bears little relation to the genuine needs of this industrial conglomeration. There are other cases in which the passion for uniformity, which is a dominating motive of all bureaucrats, whether in the Government, the unions or among employers, may well have mixed consequences. The reform of the wage structure in mining is a case in point, where both national and local bargaining is involved.

The National Coal Board, in conjunction with the unions concerned, has carried through a complete revision of the 'day-wage-men's' rate structure. This was a complicated task, since there were more than 6,000 job classifications to be examined. The same jobs were often described by different words, but to make matters more difficult the same word was also used to mean an entirely different thing in different coalfields. When all these jobs had been sorted and reclassified it was possible to reduce the total from 6,500 to 400 separate categories, which were finally grouped into thirteen main grades. Here, then, was a case in which an approach from the angle of the whole industry was fruitful and possible because there was a single employer and one union representing an overwhelming proportion of the members. These conditions are rare in British industry; the usual picture is a complex of employers and unions.

The National Coal Board and the unions still face their most formidable task, which is to rationalize the piece-rate structure affecting almost one half of the employees. It is among piece-rate workers that most of the disputes in the mining industry occur. This is not surprising, since the conditions of employment at the coal face are as variable and unpredictable as any that could be imagined. This situation is precisely the opposite from that which is generally regarded as ideal for piece-rate work, namely stable conditions and repetitive operations capable of being organized into a smooth and rhythmic flow. The problem of applying piece-rating under conditions of this kind is exposed by the demands of the miners for compensatory allowances whenever the men are unable to reach their expected norms. Not surprisingly, there has developed a tradition of bargaining not only over tasks and rates, but also over allowances. The effect of these local negotiations has been a continuous creep in allowances, which the Board is anxious to control, and the creation of friction which has resulted in many thousands of stoppages in the past decade. The abolition of the present methods would eliminate a potent cause of friction, but it is doubtful whether the problem could be effectively dealt with by way of any nationally determined uniform system of wage rates. It would be possible to substitute day-rates for the present piece-rates and greatly improve the level of supervision, but room would have to be left for local adjustment. Any attempt to impose a national rate could only succeed at a tremendous cost. The alternative would be to devise a new and better system of pit-by-pit wage settlement. Whatever changes are finally made, far more supervision and leadership at the local level will be required on the part of management and unions than has been the case hitherto. In other words, there must be a reconciliation between national control and local initiative and responsibility.

If the system of collective bargaining is to handle the problems discussed in this book with the necessary vigour, imagination and responsibility, it is essential that the unions, employers and Government should foster its development in the right direction. What is required from the Government is an economic policy which keeps the economy on an even keel without inflation and without massive unemployment. As a general rule the Government should stay out of the field of wage fixing. It may, at a highly critical moment, have to intervene because it is itself an employer of some magnitude, but its policy should normally be to follow rather than to lead, to guide rather than to dictate.

Whether free collective bargaining is to survive as the principal method by which wages and other conditions of employment are determined will depend to a large extent on the policy followed by the trade unions. At the present moment they have not completely cleared their minds on the kind of economic environment they desire. They appear to have dropped total nationalization as a goal, but they still seem to set great store by full economic planning, which can only be carried out if a vast array of controls are adopted in order to make it effective. If the state were to become the main employer, then it would be compelled to have a national wage policy and to exercise detailed as well as general control over wage changes. Since a national wages policy of this kind would mean the subjugation of the unions' freedom to bargain, as has been the case in the Soviet Union, it could not be acceptable to free trade unions. The basic objective of trade unionism, that of protecting the interest of its members, sets a practical limit to nationalization, to controls and to planning. Free labour requires free trade unions and free employers; both parties must be free, that is, to accept the responsibility of protecting and fostering their own sectional interests and at the same time the interests of the general public. It is with these fundamental issues in mind that in the last resort wages policy must be tested.

From this it follows that the union of the unions, the Trades Union Congress, has a vital role to play. Its function should not be to co-ordinate the wage policies of its affiliated unions in a strictly formal sense; in any case it does not possess the authority to do this. But if its staff were augmented and the prestige of its leadership enhanced it might give more effective guidance than it has been able hitherto. The ability of the TUC to give the kind of leadership that is required does depend to a very great extent on the willingness of the affiliated unions to recognize the need for the most objective analysis of the economic situation. Until they can be persuaded that this is in the best interests of their members and the community, the British trade union movement will not be able to make its maximum contribution to the solution of major economic and social problems.

Finally, it must be added that the employers have also a duty to play their part in making collective bargaining compatible with the maintenance of full employment, the maximum rate of economic growth, stable prices and a fair distribution of income. A constructive approach to wage problems demands something more than a mere negative opposition to the claims of the unions. It demands that employers should have a dynamic approach to industrial relations; that they should vigorously pursue a policy of increasing efficiency, and of seeking higher profits by higher turnover rather than by raising prices. If the positive approach to industrial relations developed by the more imaginative concerns were to be extended over the whole field of industry it would go a long way towards creating the climate of understanding that would make a solution to the problems discussed in this book much easier to achieve.

INDEX

THE END

For Product Safety Concerns and Information please contact our
EU representative GPSR@taylorandfrancis.com Taylor & Francis
Verlag GmbH, Kaufingerstraße 24, 80331 München, Germany